# ANATOMY OF FOUR RACE RIOTS

# Anatomy of Four Race Riots

## RACIAL CONFLICT IN KNOXVILLE, ELAINE (ARKANSAS), TULSA AND CHICAGO, 1919–1921

*by*
LEE E. WILLIAMS
*and*
LEE E. WILLIAMS II

*Foreword by Roy Wilkins*

UNIVERSITY AND COLLEGE PRESS
OF MISSISSIPPI

1972

Copyright © 1972 by
The University and College Press of Mississippi
Library of Congress Catalog Card Number 72–76856
ISBN Number 0–87805–009–4
Manufactured in the United States of America
Designed by J. Barney McKee

THIS VOLUME IS AUTHORIZED
AND SPONSORED BY
JACKSON STATE COLLEGE
JACKSON, MISSISSIPPI

# PREFACE

This book presents a general picture of several racial riots against black people. An introductory work, it presupposes no extensive technical knowledge of the riots under study on the part of the reader. The psychological, economic, sociological, and human matrix problems encountered in the study of riots are often complex, and the book makes no attempt at false over-simplification. At the same time, every effort has been made to give proper emphasis and clarity of presentation so that the general reader should be able to follow the narrative successfully.

The work emphasizes strongly those aspects of American nationalism that relate closely to the fundamental structure of black-white relations and the social order. For example, it deals with riots in the big city and the small town. It devotes about equal attention to the economic and sexual motivations that spark racial outbreaks. The work looks optimistically, but skeptically, at the "New Negro" era keeping the present in mind. We feel that the knowledge of this part of the black experience, with emphasis upon white actions and not primarily black reactions, will prove invaluable in the present struggle. As aptly pointed out in another study, custom and law removed black people from the American middle class and from access to it. As a group they earned the smallest incomes, suffered the severest ostracisms, worked in the meanest occupations, received the worst educations, and competed for the narrowest opportunities. Indeed the alienation and anger that poor whites had vented in the protest movements of the 1890's, movements which enlisted Afro-Americans in a common cause, were expressed after the Great War largely in hostility toward black people.

The post-World War I world broke in upon the consciousness of the Afro-American in a way that the white man could never experience. For most Americans it was a time of weariness and reaction against noble sentiments, a time of artificially induced superpatriotism, a time of dissillusionment, a time of fear—fear of dimly perceived forces that heralded change. For the black American, says S. P. Fullinwider, "it was a time of shock, a time of high hopes smashed to rubble." Black men had marched to war in the belief that new forces were working for democracy. They marched back home knowing they had been wrong. Black people returned to racial riots and lynchings. But blacks of postwar America were restless; and, as the riots proved, in certain areas they became aggressive, even belligerent.

As will be seen, these riots and others, were reactions by whites against the new spirit of black people. This revulsion was a direct result of the postwar spirit on the part of the white majority to keep the democratic excesses of the European theater from spilling over into this white man's country. Whites ventured in America to keep this country safe by preventing democratic idealism and actualization from existing here for black people. Black people—especially the returning black war veteran—felt, if not for the first time, that they deserved better from the white citizens of their respective communities. They learned all too tragically that racial bigotry had not subsided in such places as Tulsa, Omaha, Elaine, Knoxville, Washington, and Chicago.

Finally, we remain indebted to numerous persons and institutions whose encouragement and assistance in this instance helped make this book possible. We are grateful to all, whose generous aid, we believe, has made this a substantially stronger work than it would have been otherwise.

LEE E. WILLIAMS AND LEE E. WILLIAMS II

The authors have studied four "race riots" and have reaffirmed the commonly held conclusion that all four were launched by whites in order to impose traditional conformity on blacks and to maintain the *status quo*. In each instance it was the Negro citizens who were the victims, and the underlying cause was racial tension between the two groups. There were, also, the authors conclude, differing reasons which played important roles in causing the conflicts.

The Elaine, Arkansas, riot (really an armed assault by whites on a Negro meeting) followed the organization of a union of black tenant farmers to end abuses and exploitation by white landlords in Phillips County. The Elaine, Arkansas, riot differs from the other three in that here was an attempt to maintain, not a social position, but economic domination. Of course, in the sense that any resistance by Southern Negroes was a disturbance of the social mores, the Arkansas violence was also "social." Two of the other three were sparked by unsubstantiated reports of attempted rape of white women by black men, and the third by racial housing friction.

The black sharecroppers in Phillips County, Arkansas, sought to raise their market income from the sale of cotton. They held a meeting in a Hoop Spur Negro church, at which a Negro lawyer from the city told them about their rights and offered to represent them in court. Whites fired into the church, Negroes fired back, and a white man was killed. Seventy-nine Negroes were indicted for first degree murder or lesser offenses. The nightmare case ended four years later in 1923, when the Supreme Court held, in *Moore* v. *Dempsey*, that due process of law was not enjoyed by the defendants because the mob spirit had invaded the trial and dictated the death sentences. All the accused men—seventy-nine—were set free through the skill of a black lawyer retained by the NAACP.

The distorted report of a white woman elevator operator triggered the racial outbreak in Tulsa, Oklahoma, on May 30, 1921. She initially told police that a nineteen-year-old Negro entered the elevator and attempted to criminally assault her. A few hours later the police found that he had accidentally stepped on her foot. The number of casualties from this riot has never been accurately determined, but according to Walter White's "Eruption of Tulsa," 50 whites and from 150 to 200 blacks would appear to be an accurate count of the deaths.

The Tulsa riot illustrates the classic lie of criminal assault which was used for decades to justify lynchings and assaults upon Negroes in both the South and the North. Helen Boardman's study "Thirty Years of Lynching," made for the NAACP, was the first systematic effort to examine the crime. She found that in only 20 percent of the lynchings was sex even mentioned; in less than 10 percent was any type of sexual relationship actually involved—not that the act itself always occurred, for in some of these it was not sexual intercourse, but such actions as passing notes or indicating a desire or intention.

The Chicago riot of 1919 lasted for four days, from July 27 to August 1. Thirty-six people were killed and 536 injured. This riot followed two years of continuous friction between the two groups which had resulted in the killing of 27 Negroes "because they dared move from their segregated blocks into neighborhoods of whites." The specific incident that ignited the riot was the drowning of a Negro who had been knocked from a raft by a rock which had been thrown by a white person whom the police refused to arrest.

In August, 1919, following World War I, as tensions between Negroes and whites increased, Knoxville, Tennessee, erupted into a period of looting and death. The immediate causes of the riot included the charges of forcible entry of a black male into the bedroom of a white woman, robbery at gun point, murder, and an unsuccessful attempt to lynch the accused. Hundreds of persons were reportedly wounded and seven were killed—six Negro citizens and one white. Twelve men and one woman, all white, were arrested as a result of the mass roundup of leaders in the assault on the jail in which the Negro prisoner was thought to be held and in the looting of stores during the riot. Thirty more whites were subsequently arrested for aiding prisoners to escape and for larceny.

Each of these riots grew from the troubled times following the World War I. This was a period in which groups fought against each other in struggles which often broke into bloody conflict. The migration of blacks to the North during the war years ended in a series of racial riots in Northern cities. Blacks on the move in the South caused whites to fear change and forced them to react with lynchings and racial wars to keep the black people from going North and in "their place." The rise of the Klan divided Americans religiously and socially and pitted rural, small-town America against urban America. Inadequate housing for Negroes, wartime intolerance, high rents, inefficiency of the police, black-white economic competition where blacks were attempting to alter their position of subordination—all were contributing factors, assert the authors.

Another important component, they assert, was the deification of the white woman. Negro men were made to appear as brutal savages, out to rape white women. The phrase "a big, burly black" became journalistic shorthand for alleged Negro sex criminality. The authors finally concluded that the whites decided that fear of white power would do more to subjugate the Negro than any other method and also that the "rape" story would save face in the international community. Violence was deemed necessary to entrench the "white-imposed" fact that black people must remain under the heel of the white benefactor and that they could not survive in this country without the white man's benevolent aid. The best way that this goal could be achieved was "to scare the black population into a psychological acceptance of anything the white father might do."

*Anatomy of Four Race Riots* concludes that "the white rioted against the black people to put the upward bound black man back into his place as the Mudsill of American Society."

Prejudice persists and no path is without its obstacles. More sophisticated restraints are employed nowadays; but if history is any indication, these, too, will be overcome. If black young people will study the history of their people in America, if they will judge the older generation by the conditions obtaining and the tools available to blacks in that era, the race can go far. In fact, it can make spectacular progress if they, unhampered by the crude intimidation, terror, and death of the riots of 1919–1921 and fortified by a new self-image, will do their share, from their 1972 platform.

Roy Wilkins
Executive Director
National Association for the
Advancement of Colored People

# CONTENTS

ANATOMY OF FOUR RACE RIOTS

# CHAPTER I

# Introduction

Black movements for change in the post-World War I period caused a reaction by whites, North and South, to impose a conformity on black people that existed during the long era of slavery. Racism, lynchings, various brutalities, and riots all served as means for the suppression of a new intellectual, economic, and political rise of the black masses that emerged during the World War I period. The segregation pattern before the war suffered many alterations while the United States fought the Great War to end all wars and to preserve the world for democracy. After the autocratic powers had been defeated, many veterans returned to find a changed America. Blacks held the whites' old jobs, lived in their residential areas, drove big cars, wore silk suits and alligator shoes, and had a completely new outlook about the way things should be in "the land of the free and the home of the brave." Whites could not understand this "new nigger," but they knew that something had to be done to put him back into his place.[1]

The psychology of racism maintained that a belief in the innate inferiority of one race or ethnic group usually coupled itself with a belief in the inferiority of all

---

[1] I. A. Newby, *Jim Crow's Defense: Anti-Negro Thought in America, 1900–30*, (Baton Rouge: Louisiana State University Press, 1967) passim.

strange or alien groups. Yet white-American racists concentrated on one group—black people—and rarely gave serious attention to others. A sudden outpouring of anti-black literature inundated the South and the nation from the 1890's to 1920. Accompanying this outpouring during the latter part of the nineteenth century, the black man's social, economic, and political status were determined by the abandonment of the race by northern politicians' bothersome questions on the Adamic creation, by neglecting Orientals and other racial groups, and even by disregarding the Christian concept of the brotherhood of man. The religious racists told the faithful that blacks were inferior and whites superior, that segregation remained righteous and discrimination just, and that by nature blacks must remain "hewers of wood and drawers of waters." [2]

White Protestant churches were segregated and segregating institutions. They tended to exemplify racial pride, and although the riots of Phillips County, Arkansas, and Tulsa, Oklahoma, took a frightful toll in life and property, the state religious conventions of Arkansas and Oklahoma and the district conventions that convened soon after the riots remained silent. Black agitators stood blamed and the whites excused for resorting to violence.[3]

[2] I. A. Newby, 83–91.
[3] Robert M. Miller, *American Protestantism and Social Issues, 1919–1939* (Chapel Hill: University of North Carolina Press, 1958), 297–300; Robert M. Miller, "The Protestant Churches and Lynching, 1919–1939," *Journal of Negro History*, XLII (1957), 119–31.

The black man became virtually friendless. Condemned to a subordinate position in nature by science
and disparaged by history for his alleged failure "to
contribute anything to man's civilization," he now
found himself abandoned, ignored, or patronized by
Christianity and the nation's religious community. To
him, the brotherhood of man remained no more mean-
ingful than the fatherhood of God. The application of
Christian precepts to racial relations meant at best that
"whites would be good to blacks and refrain from
lynching or otherwise physically abusing them." In return blacks were expected, and required for their own
good, to be "faithful, happy, humble and ingratiating."
In this way only could blacks hope for eternal heav-
enly salvation. As for life on this earth, "black servants must obey their white masters." When black people became restless and impatient with subordination,
whites reacted instinctively against them, but their fury
would subside when the restlessness diminished. Thus
racial relations, although generally tranquil, sometimes
erupted violently. Their nature at any time, however,
"depended solely upon black people and their willingness to remain subordinate." The "country darky,"
furthermore, had always been overawed by threats or
occasional acts of violence, but the articulate, literate,
and independent members of the urban black middle
class that emerged around the 1920's did not genuflect
to these threats or violent actions. This class clearly became a threat to the *status quo*, and many whites des-

perately sought either to impede or to stop its growth.[4]

Undoubtedly, much of the hatred of black people which broke out in the form of lynching parties and racial riots stemmed from the fact that after 1865 the black race became the "symbol of defeat" in the Civil War and the symbol of exploitation during Reconstruction. Caught up in their emotions of terror and despair, lynchings and rioting were for many whites attempts to regain self-assurance by performing "the ritual of white supremacy." Racial hatred magnified black people's offenses, whether serious or trivial, and a "quick and passionate resentment" by whites grew out of this hatred against any move on the part of blacks toward equality. The unreasoning fear of black people by whites, especially in the South, provides a logical explanation of the hatred that whites held for blacks. The widely held belief that black men were more prone to give vent to their "animal passions," especially against whites, struck terror in the hearts of many whites, in the North and South alike.[5] Then too, World War I aroused in black people a new hope for restoration of their rights and a new militancy in demanding first-class citizenship. Temporary prosperity also gave blacks new hopes and desires that needed fulfillment, and official propaganda picturing American participation in the war as a crusade for democracy raised the natural de-

[4] Newby, 109–22.
[5] John S. Ezell, *The South Since 1865* (New York: The Macmillan Company, 1963), 361–62.

mand for a little more democracy at home. But the war-bred hopes of black people for first-class citizenship were quickly smashed in a reaction of rioting and violence that was unprecedented.[6]

It is clear that most black soldiers resented being denied certain privileges enjoyed by their white counterparts. They felt that since they were equally called on to fight when the country faced danger, they should be equally privileged when the country was safe. Since World War I exposed thousands of black soldiers to truly democratic conditions overseas, "uppity" returning black veterans aroused mounting hostility from whites. As members of this subordinate group were increasingly urbanized, skilled, and educated, the level of protest and dissatisfaction increased. More and more black people, particularly the educated elite, came to challenge openly the "place" assigned to them by the dominant group and to question the legitimacy of the entire system. Terrorism and rioting resulted.

Stereotypes of black people changed from the humble, happy-go-lucky "good nigger" or "native" who "knew his place" to the "cheeky, uppity, insolent, treacherous, sly, violent new black man or detribalized scum" who threatened the *status quo*. In the North their new footholds in industry were contested by anxious white job-seeking veterans. A wave of lynchings swept the South, and even more bloody racial riots swept the

[6] C. Vann Woodward, *The Strange Career of Jim Crow* (New York: Oxford University Press, 1957), 100.

North. Without doubt the accumulated experiences during and immediately after the war came as a severe shock to the blacks and had lasting effects since they had had to fight desperately for the right to fight for their country in the war.[7]

The war ended, and the black soldiers returned home. Blacks noted their treatment on the railroads, all of which were under government control. Many of these men going home with laurels of victory won in their country's defense were not permitted to ride in other than Jim Crow cars. Many were assaulted and thrown off the cars by government officials simply because of their color. Some were immediately stripped of their uniforms and forced to put on overalls at railroad stations in the South. Others met death because they sought equal treatment with whites. Distrust reawakened and rumors sprang up everywhere. Suspicion and fear took a deep hold on both races, and mob violence broke out. In city after city racial riots flamed up, resulting in casualties on both sides.[8]

The spirit of the black man who crossed the oceans, who saw action, and who went "over the top" was by

[7] E. E. Miller, "The War And Race Feeling," *Outlook*, CXXIII (September 10, 1919), 52; Pierre L. van den Berghe, *Race and Racism: A Comparative Perspective* (New York: John Wiley and Sons, 1967), 92–128; Gunnar Myrdal, *An American Dilemma: The Negro Problem and Modern Democracy* (New York: Harper and Brothers, 1944), 745 and 1005.

[8] Chicago *Defender*, April 5, 1919; W. S. Scarborough, "Race Riots and Their Remedy," *Independent and Weekly Review*, XCIX (August 16, 1919), 223; 1409.

no means the spirit of the black man before the war; for the black man who fought underwent a metamorphosis of mind that produced an altogether new man, with new ideas, new hopes, and new aspirations. He would not quietly submit to former conditions without a vigorous protest.[9] Thus the war caused a vital change in the position of black people and in their own feeling about their position. In the southern states the black community contributed almost as many men as did the whites. They bought Liberty Bonds, subscribed to the Red Cross and other funds, and played their part in the crisis as did whites. After the war they felt the opportunity for life, liberty, and the pursuit of happiness accorded them was in some sense a "supreme test of this country's professions." If the white man tried to "show the nigger his place" by flogging, lynching, and rioting against him, the black man, when the government did not defend him, "would purchase arms to defend himself."[10]

In a number of southern newspapers there appeared a disposition to "crow" over the disorders of the North and to point "the finger of scorn" at those northern critics who had condemned mob violence, lynching, and, in general, the treatment of blacks in the South. Many letters written to northern newspapers predicted that, as a consequence of disorders, the North would

[9] Scarborough, 223; see app. A.
[10] *The Johnson City* (Tennessee) *Staff*, May 14, 1919; Herbert J. Seligmann, "Race War in Washington," *New Republic*, XX (August 13, 1919), 50.

have to learn to deal with racial problems "as they have been dealt with in the South . . . ." They evidently approved of "the sport in torture." Page one of the *Vicksburg Evening Post* recounted the murder of Lloyd Clay and quoted a leader as saying, "Have you had enough fun boys? Yes, cut him down." [11]

Rape was apparently the best available defense of lynching, and lynching became the most powerful and convincing form of racial repression until the advent of racial rioting. Lynching may be defined as "an act of homicidal aggression" committed by one people against another through mob action to "suppress either some tendency in the latter from an accommodated position of subordination or for subjugation further to some lower social status." It served the function of providing whites with the means of "periodically reaffirming their collective sentiment of white dominance." In addition, the lynch mob would be composed of whites who had been "carefully indoctrinated" by the primary social institutions of a given region to conceive of black people as "extra-legal, extra-democratic objects" without rights that white people had to respect. Lynchings were not the work of men suddenly possessed of a strange madness. They were "the logical issues of prejudice and lack of respect for law and personality," and lynchers identified themselves in order to be glorified.

[11] Herbert J. Seligmann, "What Is Behind the Negro Uprisings?" *Current Opinion*, LXVII (September, 1919), 154; Herbert J. Seligmann, "Protecting Southern Womanhood," *Nation*, CVIII (June 14, 1919), 938; see app. A.

Both the overt threat of lynching and unsuccessful lynchings functioned to maintain white dominance. They provided the "socio-psychological matrix of the power relationship between the races."[12]

The lynching cycle included, first, a growing belief among whites in the area that blacks were "getting out of hand," and the development of a "summatory attitude" of racial antagonism. Next, the rumored, or actual, occurrence of some outrage by a black upon a white or group of whites led to a white mob apprehending a black and lynching him. This reprisal drove all blacks under cover, for they became intimidated and terrified. Finally, there appeared a new interracial adjustment whereby the thoroughly frightened blacks began to "smile broadly and ingratiatingly" over the merest whim of the whites to show that they bore "no malice for the horrible past." The cycle was then set to begin anew. Lynching, therefore, has regularly been a means of social control that consists of taking the lives of one or more persons by mob action in retribution for some criminal or social offense.[13]

Lynchings occurred mostly in those areas in which the laws discriminated against blacks and in which the judicature facilitated such acts. Furthermore, the lynching attitude could be found "everywhere among whites in the United States." Despite the southerners' use of

[12] Oliver C. Cox, "Lynching and the Status Quo," *Journal of Negro Education*, XIV (1945), 577–84.
[13] *Ibid.*, 576–78.

lynching as a preventive of rape, a brief submitted to Congress by the National Association for the Advancement of Colored People stated that of 3,224 persons lynched in America between 1889 and 1918, only 523 were accused of rape.[14]

Past rationalizations of lynching have comprised notions that the black man is by nature criminally inclined, and that periodic lynchings were necessary to keep him under control; that criminal justice is slow and uncertain; and that particularly abhorrent crimes produced "spontaneous reactions" on the part of an outraged citizenry. In addition, there were six patterns of interracial social violence in the period between 1915 and 1929 which were different enough in characteristics to be identified as: lynching; mutiny and insurrection; individual interracial assaults and homicides; racial arson and bombings; "southern style" racial riots; and "northern style" racial riots.[15]

The role of economic competition was indirectly seen in that lynchings were most frequent in areas that had been recently settled, where rivalry for jobs was keen, and where long-established mores had not clearly

[14] *Ibid.*, 576–77; Herbert J. Seligmann, "The Menace Of Race Hatred," *Harper's Monthly Magazine*, CXL-CXLI (1920), 742; Ben R. Rogers, "William E. B. DuBois, Marcus Garvey And Pan-Africa," *Journal of Negro History*, XL (1955), 154.

[15] George E. Simpson and J. Milton Yinger, *Racial and Cultural Minorities* (New York: Harper and Brothers, 1958), 516; Allen D. Grimshaw, "Lawlessness and Violence in America and Their Special Manifestations in Changing Negro-White Relationships," *Journal of Negro History*, XLIV (1959), 65.

defined the expected status of racial groups. They characteristically occurred in small towns or in rural areas below the economic average where contact with the law and with outside ideas and information were meager. Furthermore, an analysis of the lynchings that occurred during any given period clearly revealed the "economic dislocations of the communities where the lynchings took place." [16]

According to Marcus Garvey, black people in America could expect oppression because the white race had "the power to oppress." Lynchings and racial rioting were not abnormal; they were to be expected. In North America, said Garvey, the black man lived "on the fringe of the civilization of others," and if he remained there, in the end "he would be completely obliterated." [17] Apparently many whites listened to Garvey and actually tried to "obliterate" blacks in the racial rioting that occurred between 1919 and 1921. The most savage oppression took place when black people refused to accept a subordinate position, and the most intense conflict resulted when the minority group attempted to disrupt "the accommodative pattern" or when the "superordinate group" defined the situation as one in which such an attempt was being made.[18] The black man's impulse toward better social and economic conditions aroused passionate and primitive resentment in

[16] Hadley Cantril, *The Psychology of Social Movements* (New York: John Wiley and Sons, 1941), 84–91.
[17] Ben R. Rogers, 159.
[18] Allen D. Grimshaw, 71.

many parts of the country, chiefly among whites who came nearest to being on the same economic plane with the mass of the black labor force.[19]

After four years of war, with atrocities on behalf of civilization and democracy exhibited on the front page of every newspaper, it is no wonder that violence should have become the order of the day. War was, in fact, organized and legalized mob action, but the mob action under discussion became all the more dangerous because it was unorganized and illegal. In addition, mob violence is immensely enjoyable for everyone except the victim who, after all, cannot expect much consideration. Ninety per cent of the people of America at this time were law-abiding and, for the most part, indifferent to the other 10 per cent who, while calling themselves 100-per-cent Americans, derived amusement from not being law-abiding. Until the 90-per-cent group of Americans remedied this major defect they had to continue fearing, not the overthrow of the government by the Reds, but by the "Red-White-and-Blues." The atmosphere of the late nineteenth century had been so thoroughly permeated with racist thought, reinforced by Darwinism, that few men managed to escape it. The idea that certain cultures and races were naturally inferior to others was almost universally held by educated, middle-class, respectable Americans—in other words, by the dominant majority. They had

[19] "Racial Tension and Race Riots," *Outlook*, CXXII (August 6, 1919), 534.

fought for principles and beliefs in the past, so why not for this one? [20]

During the summer of 1919, there were some twenty-five racial outbreaks, with the largest occurring in Chicago, Illinois. Others sprang up in 1920 and 1921, with the Tulsa, Oklahoma, riot taking the heaviest toll in life and property. There were two basic types of riots. The first was the chiefly "sentimental or passional" riot exemplified in Knoxville, Tennessee, and Tulsa, occurring most frequently in the South. The second was the predominantly "business or economic riot," of which Chicago and Elaine, Arkansas, were typical. The blacks' pride in their increasing prosperity as a result of the war and their willingness to fight for their rights intensified racial hatred among whites throughout the South and North. Racial riots against black people thus became instruments for the completion of this reaction.[21]

Racial rioting originated in a state of mind and in public opinion. The lack of friendly contacts between the races in the local community, sensational newspaper publicity, and the changes in the feelings and thoughts of blacks were also paramount factors in racial riots. The changes in occupations and wages brought more

[20] "Law-And-Order Anarchy," *Nation*, CXIII (August 13, 1921), 113; Christopher Lasch, "The Anti-Imperialists, The Philippines, and the Inequality of Man," *Journal of Southern History*, XXIV (1958), 330; see app. A.
[21] Seligmann, "Negro Uprisings?" 154; Ben R. Rogers, 154; Arthur I. Waskow, *From Race Riot to Sit-in: 1919 and the 1960's* (New York: Doubleday, 1966), 13.

of the material satisfactions of life to black people and spurred their desire for higher standards of living. The migration to the North showed blacks that liberty allowed a man to move more freely from place to place. It taught them that their change of residence need not be attended with a loss of opportunity to make a living, or with any danger of suffering from the climate or from the strangeness of a new land. This emerging understanding of the meaning of liberty was driven deep into the consciousness of the black masses, and so they assumed a new attitude when they were in contact with the white community. The new experiences occurring in the migration north, in the war service, and in the new economic opportunities developed a new type of black man. But thousands of whites also migrated to the North, and when blacks competed with them for the same jobs and residential areas, friction ensued.[22]

Several other factors helped foment riot situations: the policy of segregation in the army; the segregation of white blood from black blood by the Red Cross, though the two types are chemically indistinguishable; and the prejudiced attitudes which provoked intolerance. Added to these factors were appropriate stimuli

[22] Edgar T. Thompson and Everett C. Hughes (eds.), Race: Individual and Collective Behavior (Glencoe, Ill.: The Free Press, 1958), 399; George E. Haynes, "Race Riots in Relation to Democracy," Survey, XLII (August 9, 1919), 698–99; Paul A. Carter, The Decline and Revival of the Social Gospel: Social and Political Liberalism in American Protestant Churches, 1920–1940 (Ithaca: Cornell University Press, 1954), 130–31.

characteristics possessed by blacks—visible distinction; strange or alien behavior; white antipathy toward blacks; interracial competition in the labor market and the political arena; attempts to drive blacks back into their ghettos; and the widespread white determination to reestablish the black man's prewar status as the mudsill of American society.[23]

Racial riots like the one in Chicago in the summer of 1919 tended to drive black people together for mutual help. Once aroused they became not only racially conscious, but also economically conscious, and from this realization blacks began to enter business on a larger scale. In every riot violence was largely one-sided and consisted of attacks, of varying degrees of organization, by whites on the black community. In all such "southern style" riots there were charges of black assaults upon white women.[24]

The immediate precipitants of racial riots almost always involve some confrontation between the groups in which members of one race are deeply "wronged" in fact or in rumor by members of the other. They tend to be transgressions of strongly held mores by a representative of the other group. Riots are often started in the United States by crimes, particularly alleged crimes against "persons rather than property alone, or the

[23] Mabel A. Elliott and Francis E. Merrill, *Social Disorganization* (New York: Harper and Brothers, 1961), 658; William B. Tuttle, Jr., "Views of a Negro During the Red Summer of 1919—A Document," *Journal of Negro History*, LI (1966), 210.
[24] J. H. Harmon, Jr., "The Negro as a Local Business Man," *Journal of Negro History*, XIV (1929), 139; Grimshaw, 67–68.

public order." Murder, rape, assault, manslaughter, and theft by means of violence or intimidation arouse the greatest concern and receive the most publicity in the mass media. At least a sizable proportion of the immediate causes of racial rioting appears to involve "interracial violations of intense societal norms," among which are the large number of events caused by bodily injury and the smaller number of cases motivated by "violations of interracial segregation taboos." [25]

According to Stanley Lieberson and Arnold R. Silverman, sources of racial rioting often include highly charged offenses committed by members of one group against another. These riots are generalized responses in which there is categorical assault on persons and property by virtue of their racial membership. Such violence is not restricted and may even exclude the specific antagonists responsible for the precipitating event. In addition, riots are likely to occur when social institutions function inadequately, when grievances are not resolved, or cannot be resolved under the existing institutional arrangements. The immediate motive simply ignites prior community tensions revolving about basic institutional difficulties. The failure of functionaries to perform the roles expected by one or both of the racial groups, cross-pressures, or the absence of an institution capable of handling of a community prob-

[25] Stanley Lieberson and Arnold R. Silverman, "The Precipitants and Underlying Conditions of Race Riots," *American Sociological Review*, XXX (1965), 888–91.

lem involving interracial relations will create the conditions under which riots are most likely to occur. Many
riots are started by offenses that arouse considerable interest and concern. Riot torn cities not only employ
fewer black policemen, but they are also communities
whose political systems tend to be less sensitive to
demands of the electorate. Furthermore, riots are more
likely where blacks are "closer to whites in their pro-
portions in traditional black occupations," and where
black-white income differences are smaller, "suggesting
that a conflict of interests between the races is inherent
in the economic world." [26]

During these particular riots under study, rumors
about specific incidents or racial strife spread by word
of mouth. Newspapers contributed to racial tension
by frequently and repeatedly publishing inflammatory
reports. Since these riots often lasted for several days,
news reports served to recruit white activists from other
parts of the city and even from out of town. Editorial
efforts to calm public opinion and to demand effective
law enforcement developed slowly and hardly bal-
anced the presentation in news columns. Furthermore,
the restoration of civil order required the police to
separate the two groups and to protect the enclaves of
blacks from whites. Frequently, the police were defi-
cient in their duties and occasionally assisted white
rioters. In any case they did not prepare for such outbreaks. The state militia or federal troops had to be

[26] *Ibid.*, 896–97.

used repeatedly. Apart from the casualties caused by the police themselves, the fundamental anatomy of these riots was a "communal clash" between blacks and whites.[27]

[27] National Commission on the Causes and Prevention of Violence, June 1969, *Violence In America* (New York: The New American Library, 1969), 396–98.

# CHAPTER II

# The
# Knoxville Riot

The tension that characterized the changed relations between blacks and whites in the immediate postwar period erupted into looting and death in late August, 1919, in Knoxville, Tennessee. The causes of the riot included the classic charges of forcible entry of a black male into a white woman's bedroom, robbery at gun point, murder, and an unsuccessful attempt to lynch the accused.

While commenting on racial antagonism in 1919, Congressman James Byrnes, democrat from South Carolina, declared in the House of Representatives that, because of the propaganda that circulated through black newspapers and magazines, antagonism between the races got out of hand.[1] The fiery Byrnes blamed politicians for trying to increase the number of black voters and designing capitalists for using blacks as strikebreakers as a means of keeping wages down.[2] Furthermore, Byrnes stated that blacks who obeyed the law could remain in the South, but that those who had been "inoculated with the desire for political equality or social equality must stay away: as there existed no

[1] Knoxville *Journal and Tribune*, August 26, 1919, 3.
[2] U.S., *Congressional Record*, LVIII (August 25–September 12, 1919), 4302.

room for these blacks in the South." The means for keeping these blacks law abiding or out of the South may be summarized as occasional lynchings and "wars" against black people, such as the Knoxville riot of 1919.[3]

The occasion for the Knoxville riot was the murder of Mrs. Bertie Lindsey at her home, 1216 Eighth Avenue, North Knoxville, about 2:20 A.M. Saturday, August 30, 1919. According to interviews printed in a local paper, Mrs. Lindsey, sleeping in the same bed with her cousin Ora Smyth, awakened to a flashing light in the room and screamed. Thereupon a man, presumed black, drew his pistol and commanded her to remain in the bed. When she attempted to rise and escape through a window, the intruder fired his gun, and the bullet passed through the woman's heart. He then fled the scene.[4]

Ora Smyth, twenty years old, became the only witness to the incident. She had been living in the house with her cousin since the early part of the year and worked at the Standard Knitting Mills, Inc. Three weeks prior to the murder, Mr. Dan W. Lindsey left for Akron, Ohio, to seek employment and he expected to move his wife to that city after finding work.[5]

In an interview with a reporter from the *Journal and Tribune*, Miss Smyth exhibited "coolness and game-

[3] *Ibid.*; Newby, *passim.*

[4] Knoxville *Journal and Tribune*, August 31, 1919.

[5] *Ibid.*; Charles R. Davenport, "The Knoxville Riot—August 30–31, 1919," Manuscript, University of Tennessee Archives, Knoxville, 1967, 1.

ness" which could hardly have been surpassed. Although she slept in the same bed with her cousin, and despite the fact that she witnessed the entire proceeding, she neither screamed nor made any motion sufficient to bring the wrath of the assailant upon herself. "If I'd moved, he'd have killed me, too," she said.[6]

Later during the interview, however, Miss Smyth showed great nervousness, frequently sobbing and crying as she recalled the details of the tragedy. Ora said that she slept "unusually well" until awakening "just before" the fatal shot. She did not awake suddenly as it took her a moment to realize that someone stood in the room; but Ora became fully awake, saw "the dim figure of a man" bending over Bertie Lindsey, and heard Bertie crying. According to Miss Smyth, Bertie was extremely frightened, so much so that the bed shook from her crying, that Bertie muttered something and begged, but her words were so stifled with crying that Ora could not understand her. The man was identified as one "who by his voice was a negro," and whom Ora recognized as a black man when the flashlight shined momentarily on his hands several times and on his face at least once. The intruder cursed and threatened to kill Mrs. Lindsey if she did not lie down. Apparently he did not see Ora in the bed.[7]

Ora Smyth described how Bertie Lindsey reached for the foot of the bed, rose, and stood between the bed

6 Knoxville *Journal and Tribune*, August 31, 1919.
7 *Ibid.*

railing and the wall. The man threatened again to kill
her. When she stepped in the direction of the window,
a shot rang out, and Bertie fell to the floor. The man left
the house by the rear door, presumably the same way
he had entered. Ora immediately ran next door to the
home of Policeman and Mrs. T. E. Dyer, and she stated
that, as she ran, she could still see "the dim shadow of a
man" going from the house toward Caswell Park. As
Ora Smyth entered the neighbors' home, the Dyers
told her that they had mistaken the shot for a "torpedo"
on the nearby railroad tracks. They failed, therefore, to
investigate.

After Ora Smyth entered the house, Mrs. Dyer saw
the man turn around and pass the home again as he had
once before passed the Lindsey home while Ora entered
the Dyer residence. The man passed the house this second time, went into an alley, and started running. According to Miss Smyth, he resembled the "same man
that had killed Bertie." Mr. Dyer called the police, who
came swiftly, and Mrs. Dyer and Miss Smyth described
the assailant to them. The officers said they recognized
the man from the women's description, a black man
called Mays.[8]

Maurice Mays may be described as the type of black
man usually referred to as "high yellow." He appeared
slender, almost frail, weighing one hundred twenty-
nine pounds and standing five feet five inches tall. "His
countenance was that of an intelligent person." He had

[8] *Ibid.*

lived in Knoxville all of his life, and he had a ninth-grade education. Mays told of the events prior to his arrest to a reporter from the *Journal and Tribune*. According to Mays, on Friday, August 29, about two o'clock in the afternoon, he and his father, William Mays, rented a buggy from the Jesse Rogers stables; and during the afternoon "canvassed the outlying suburbs of the city in behalf of Mayor McMillan." Around eight o'clock that evening they returned the buggy to the Rogers's stables, and Mays and his father parted. Mays went to Central Street and spent part of the evening talking with friends and then wandered until midnight from place to place along Vine Avenue. At this time he began looking for Jim Massengill, a black chauffeur and a close friend. During this search he at one time passed a patrolman named Bearden, "he walking down one side of the street, I on the other." After a short while, Mays met Massengill, although not until he had met several other friends. Mays got into Massengill's car, and they drove out onto Willow Street, back to East Jackson Avenue, and got out of the car at the Boston Cafe, near the corner of Central and Vine. At the Boston Cafe, Mays made an effort to call Alice Brice, another friend, but did not reach her. Mays next went to the Boyd Cafe, but found it closed. He then walked to his room at 213 Hume Street, less than two blocks from the Boyd Cafe, where he immediately undressed, got into bed, and after a short while, went to sleep. Mays said it was then about one o'clock, Saturday morning. Sometime later, Mays awoke to a light being flashed through his window. After he had awaked, he went to the door, opened it, and found policemen standing there. The officers told him that he was under arrest and ordered him to get dressed. As Mays dressed the officers searched his room and found in his bureau drawer a thirty-eight-calibre "lemon squeezer" made by Smith and Wesson. Mays told the officers that he had had the gun for almost three years, and that the gun had not been fired for some time.[9]

The officers took Mays back to the scene of the crime to be identified and for him to look at the dead woman. At the scene they placed Mays under a street lamp, and Ora Smyth "identified him positively as the negro who killed Bertie." Mrs. T. E. Dyer told the officers that Mays "looked like" the man who had passed in front of her home. The officers thereupon took Mays to the Knox County jail. Hundreds of persons visited the scene of the crime on Saturday until late in the afternoon. Small groups of men congregated on practically every street corner and near every store in the neighborhood to discuss the crime.[10]

Police Chief Haynes and other members of the police department soon became convinced that Mays had

---

[9] Ibid.

[10] Ibid.; Mays at one time had served as deputy sheriff under Sheriff Callaway. While serving as deputy sheriff, Mays had killed John Boyd, a Knoxville youth. The circumstances behind this incident were not revealed. Ten days prior to the Lindsey murder the police had picked up Mays on suspicion of entering a white woman's home.

entered the rooms of white women for some time. Only a few nights prior to the murder of Bertie Lindsey a man entered the home of a white woman in the Ninth Ward, and her description of the marauder tallied with that of Mays. While no clues pointed to Mays as the guilty man, police officers stated that Mays had been under surveillance for the past few weeks.[11]

Around four o'clock Saturday afternoon small groups of people began milling about the Knox County jail. At four different intervals the men chose committees and, with the permission of the jailer, went through the jail to search for Mays and to satisfy their curiosity. He could not be found because Sheriff W. T. Cate had taken him by train to the jail in Chattanooga, Tennessee, for safe keeping. Despite receiving the reports of the different committees, the mob became riotous and began shooting. As night fell a large mob, estimated at one thousand persons, decided to storm the jail, seize Mays, and lynch him. The shouting and shooting continued, and the rioters pounded on the heavy iron bars of one of the front windows until it eventually gave way. Men swarmed into the jail and overpowered the jailer and his deputies. Heavy timbers were brought and passed from hand to hand over the heads of the mob. Using these timbers as battering rams, the rioters attempted to force the doors leading to the

11 Knoxville *Journal and Tribune*, August 31, 1919. Police Chief Haynes said that Mays's gun had been fired recently because no lint was found in the barrel; see app. B.

cells containing the white prisoners. They made no attempt to free black prisoners. Failing with these timbers, the mob used guns and dynamite to break the locks.[12]

After both the doors to the jail and the doors to the cells had been blown down, the rioters released all the white prisoners confined on the upper floors. While some men released prisoners, others looted the jail. They took all the whiskey and guns they could find and broke all the windows. They destroyed all property that could not be taken. These men also stole the clothing of the jailer's children.[13]

The jailer called the mayor and informed him of the situation. Mayor John E. McMillan requested National Guardsmen to quell the disturbance. The first soldiers who arrived on the scene, sixteen men and one officer, were assaulted by the rioters, who stripped some of the soldiers of their uniforms and beat eight of them badly. One hour later one hundred and fifty more soldiers arrived. While the jail continued to be stormed about midnight Saturday, a report reached the officers in charge of the troops that several holdups had been perpetrated by an organized and heavily armed band of blacks near Vine Avenue and Central Street, the heart of the black section of Knoxville. An officer ordered a platoon to the scene, and a large portion of the mob

[12] *New York Times*, September 1, 1919 1, 4; *Nashville Banner*, August 31, 1919; Davenport, 1.
[13] *New York Times*, September 1, 1919, 1, 4.

followed the soldiers up the hill. Soon after the troops reached Gay Street two civilians and one soldier dashed up to the officer in command and reported that two soldiers had been held up and later killed at the same corner. The officer gave the command of "double time," and the soldiers advanced on the run. Their followers jumped into passing cars and trucks, which headed north on Gay Street. As the soldiers advanced, their crowd of followers increased, with several waving guns in the air and all shouting as they ran.[14]

In the meantime members of the mob made raids upon pawn shops and hardware stores. They crashed plate-glass windows, forced locks, and, in some cases, knocked doors from their hinges in an effort to secure weapons of any kind. Damage done to the stores totaled $50,000. Several furniture stores also suffered break-ins and stood looted of their stocks of kitchen knives, cleavers, and fireplace pokers. Possibly the wholesale firm of C. M. McClung and Company, located on Jackson Avenue, suffered the heaviest loss. At least one hundred men entered the building through a broken window and took every shotgun, rifle, and pistol, plus large amounts of ammunition. While the raid progressed a gun accidentally discharged with the bullet striking a sprinkler cap and causing the room to be flooded with water. Thousands of dollars worth of fur-

14 *Ibid.*, 4; Davenport, 2. The soldiers of the Fourth Tennessee National Guard were on maneuvers and camped at Chilhowee Park and Camp Sevier in southeast Knoville and just south of Knoxville, respectively; see app. B.

niture and dry goods became damaged by the water, which could not be stopped for several hours. Uncle Sam's shooting gallery suffered unlawful entry after someone shattered a glass door, but all the target rifles had been removed. The loan office of J. C. Kenner, 123 Gay Street, endured a terrible fate. The only guns left in stock happened to be three single-shot Springfield rifles that had been used in action in the Civil War. As soon as Kenner arrived upon the scene he placed a sign in the window that read: "No More Guns and Ammunition. All Gone." Rioters broke the glass doors of the Wright-Cruze Hardware Company, 213 Gay Street, but little loss occurred. This firm carried a very small stock of guns and ammunition and no pistols. The Sterling-Crumbliss Company, 320 Gay Street, appeared completely gutted of its stock of guns and ammunition. The men broke down both doors of Uncle Sam's loan office, 329 Gay Street, and stole about three hundred guns and pistols and several thousand rounds of ammunition. Many seized brass knuckles, blackjacks, and razors. The mob entered the Woodruff Hardware Company, 426 Gay Street, and a large number of high-grade guns and rifles fell into the hands of looters, who also took searchlights and cartridges. After a demand had been made for the keys, thieves broke into the store of S. B. Luttrell and Company, 613 Gay Street, and took a number of knives. At the House-Hassen wholesale hardware establishment, looters entered and stole a large stock of guns and ammunition.

The Lowe-Horde Hardware Company, at the corner of Wall Avenue and Market Street, appeared looted of several guns and about 3,000 rounds of ammunition. Another raid went awry at the Market Harness and Hardware Company, 13 Market Square, which specialized in farm implements and harnesses and carried no guns in stock.[15]

Raids continued to be made on the Bard-Cate, Bohannan Furniture, Potter Furniture, and Maxwell Furniture companies, located on Vine Avenue between Clay and Central Streets, following the first shots on Central Street. Thieves removed every implement that could be used as a weapon from these stores, and stocks were badly damaged during hasty searches. Many other windows in this section became targets for "flying lead." The only evidence that blacks broke into an establishment was found at 102 Central Street. This establishment, a second-hand store, had its stock badly upset by the raiders. The extent of the loss and damage at this store could not be determined.[16]

As the troops and the crowd rounded the corner of Gay Street and Vine Avenue and moved toward the intersection of Central Street, an automobile approached with its driver apparently unaware of any "lurking danger." Upon reaching the corner the car met shots from the building at the intersection. The driver swerved his car to the right and returned the

[15] Knoxville *Journal and Tribune*, September 1, 1919, 2.
[16] *Ibid.*

fire at once. He fired several shots into a window as he swung the car around with his other hand. As the driver made the turn he emptied his gun down Central Street. "Tongues of flame" spurted from every window as the automobile headed back up Vine Avenue. As the driver passed the troops, he waved his arm towards the corner and shouted something about "blacks being barricaded" at the end of the street. The troops halted and loaded their guns. While doing so snipers fired at them from the end of the street.[17]

Following the preliminary shooting, the troops lined up along the north side of the street to await orders. As the civilians returned from their looting expeditions, they took up positions along the street and at the heads of alleys to hold them against possible attacks. The men appeared armed with every kind of weapon from ten-gauge shotguns to air rifles, which they had secured from the raids upon the Gay Street stores. Snipers concealed in the buildings at the foot of the street fired at men in the streets constantly, but their aim was "so poor that no one was wounded." Both groups exchanged shots from time to time at each end of the street. Shots continued to be exchanged when the riot squad from the police station arrived in a touring car. They were not fired upon by the snipers until they jumped from the car and scattered along the sides of the buildings.

[17] *New York Times*, September 1, 1919, 4; Knoxville *Journal and Tribune*, September 1, 1919, 2.

One of the officers appeared to be slightly wounded in his leg, but no other casualties resulted.[18]

Shortly after the riot squad arrived, a second automobile containing two machine guns and their crews of soldiers dashed down the street and came to a stop near the corner of State Street. By this time the gunfire had ceased, and the soldiers were able to set up their machine guns without meeting resistance from the end of the street. They mounted one of the guns at each side of the street, in such a position as to command the entire street by cross fire. Lieutenant James W. Payne and two other officers advanced ahead of the guns to determine the range and the lay of the area. The officers advanced almost to the corner of Central Street by creeping along the sides of the buildings, then they moved over to the edge of the sidewalk. Lieutenant Payne stayed at a telephone pole while the other officers headed back to the machine guns. Hardly had they reached the guns when several snipers opened fire upon Lieutenant Payne. Someone shouted "Let 'em have it," and the soldiers began firing both machine guns, sending a shower of lead into the dark section of the street. The positions of the guns placed Lieutenant Payne in the range of the sweeping fire. Everyone's attention focused on the snipers, and not until after the shooting had ceased did soldiers find Lieutenant Payne mortally wounded, killed by the machine-gun fire.[19]

[18] *New York Times*, September 1, 1919, 4.
[19] *Ibid.*

More troops arrived from Camp Sevier just outside the city. This group of Fourth Tennessee National Guardsmen, under the command of Adjutant General E. B. Sweeney of Nashville and Colonel Ewing Carruthers of Memphis, quickly sprang into action, supplemented by two hundred special policemen and seventy-five special deputy sheriffs. Several shots came from snipers, troops, and civilians from each end of Central Street, but heavy firing did not resume until the snipers started shooting at a small group of civilians who crossed the street. This became the "signal for the rattle of firearms from the street." One of the machine guns opened fire again. "The excitement was increasing with every shot," and additional heavily armed civilians arrived when troops and policemen started to clear the streets. Several civilian leaders called for volunteers to follow them in an attempt to storm the barricaded blacks at the end of the street, but army officers intervened in time to prevent such attempts. Soldiers finally pushed the crowd back up the Gay Street hill, and several hundred army troops and special policemen surrounded the black section of Central Street and Vine Avenue. Early Sunday morning, August 31, things quieted down considerably, and only a few minor incidents occurred during the latter part of the day and into the night.[20]

Untold hundreds were wounded and seven persons lost their lives. James Henson, a black man, seems to

[20] *Nashville Banner*, August 31, 1919.

have been the first victim of the rioting after the action shifted from the jail.[21] Joseph Etter, black proprietor of a large second-hand store, had been shot down in the rioting on East Jackson Avenue. Nelson Easley, a black war veteran who won praise for distinguished service in overseas assignments with the American expeditionary forces, dropped dead at the home of a friend from heart trouble probably "superinduced by excitement of the racial troubles." [22] Lieutenant James W. Payne of the Fourth Tennessee National Guard appeared to be the only white man killed in the affair.

Many blacks began to leave the city Sunday afternoon. Most of them carried their worldly possessions in suitcases, trunks, and other containers. They sought the thoroughfares leading out of Knoxville and the transportation centers. By September 6, 1919, possibly more than fifteen hundred blacks had fled Knoxville for destinations in Indiana, Wisconsin, and Illinois.[23]

Police arrested twelve men and one woman, all white, as a result of the mass roundup of leaders in the assault on the jail and in the looting of stores during the riot. Jail officials believed Jeff Claiborne to be one of the leaders and the person directly responsible for the storming of the jail. Each, placed under $2,000 bond, insisted that he had had no part in releasing the prisoners and that he had entered the jail long after the bars

[21] Davenport, 3; Memphis *Commercial Appeal*, August 31, 1919.
[22] Knoxville *Journal and Tribune*, September 1, 1919.
[23] Chicago *Defender*, September 6, 1919.

had been battered down. Each said that he only acted as thousands of others would have done "under the same circumstances," and did not believe himself guilty of committing a crime. Eventually police arrested more than thirty persons for larceny or for aiding prisoners to escape.[24]

Because of a reversible error committed in the trial in the Criminal Court of Knox County, with Judge A. R. Nelson presiding, Mays received a new trial. The error was that "the jury did not undertake to assess to punishment in their verdict." They simply returned a verdict of guilty of murder in the first degree, and the court affixed the death penalty. According to the Tennessee Criminal Code, in first-degree murder cases, "the jury must return the verdict and affix said punishment." Thus the case was reversed and remanded for a new trial. Mays was again convicted in the second trial, and the Tennessee Supreme Court upheld the conviction on another appeal. Mays was then committed to the custody of the warden of the state penitentiary until December 15, 1921, at which time he was put to death by electrocution.[25]

The city of Knoxville slowly returned to normal. Maurice Mays was tried, convicted, and executed for

[24] Knoxville *Journal and Tribune*, September 2, 1919; see app. B.
[25] *Maurice Mays* v. *The State*, 143 Tenn. 16, (1920), 443–51, and 145 Tenn. 18 (1920), 118–47, in Frank M. Thompson, *Reports of Cases Argued and Determined in the Supreme Court of Tennessee* (Columbia, Mo.: E. W. Stephens Publishing Company, 1921 and 1922), vols. CXLIV and CXLV.

the murder of Bertie Lindsey. The good white citizenry of Knoxville had made its point: No "uppity nigra" will ever deflower or murder the pride of the noble South and get away with it; and furthermore, "our nigras *know* their places and . . . they had best *stay* in them." [26] [italics added]

[26] Newby, *passim.*

# CHAPTER III

# The Elaine Riot

The changes that the World War I brought to America affected even sharecroppers in the delta country of Arkansas. Blacks dared to exercise their American right to protest the traditional pattern of economic exploitation by white landlords. This decision produced a violent reaction among the whites that culminated in a concerted effort to kill or drive from the area all blacks suspected of involvement in the protest.

Phillips County, Arkansas, in 1910, had a population of 34,000, three-fourths of which was black. In one township there lived only one white man; in another, not even one resided.[1] On the east the county is bordered by the Mississippi River, separating it from the state of Mississippi; on the south by Desha County; on the west by the counties of Arkansas and Monroe; and on the north by Lee County. In the area, rich delta land abounds. People called this section the "Black Belt" because of the high concentration of black people.[2] Most of these people worked as sharecroppers on the many plantations in the region, and out of this situation burst the so-called "Elaine Riot," which occurred in early October, 1919.[3]

[1] *New York World*, November 19, 1919. U.S., *Congressional Record*, LVIII (November 19, 1919), 8819.

[2] O. A. Rogers, Jr., "The Elaine Race Riots of 1919," *Arkansas Historical Quarterly*, XIX (1960), 143.

[3] *Ibid*.; Walter F. White, "Race Conflict in Arkansas," *Survey*, XLIII (December 13, 1919), 234; see app. C.

The Gerard B. Lambert Company of St. Louis, Missouri, owned the cotton lands around the small town of Elaine.[4] Into this section in the spring and summer of 1919 came "a short, thin, very black man wearing a frock coat." The man, Robert L. Hill, twenty-six years old, hailed from Winchester, Arkansas, where he lived with his wife on a small tenant farm.[5] Hill saw that black tenant farmers needed protection from unscrupulous white landlords and decided to do something about the situation.

The blacks had had trouble getting settlements for the cotton they raised on land owned by whites. Both owner and tenant farmer supposedly shared the profits from the yearly sale, but the owner began selling the crop whenever and however he saw fit. At the time of settlement, in most cases, the blacks received no itemized statement nor cottonseed-money account. Only the total amount owed appeared in the records, followed by a settlement which kept many blacks indebted to the landlord. The blacks feared protesting against this disadvantageous system because of intimidation and possible bodily harm. Alleged abuses of padding and peonage by unscrupulous landlords and their agents became common, but most blacks remained helpless in defending themselves. Many black tenant farmers in Phillips County did not get a settlement be-

[4] *New York World*, November 19, 1919. U.S. *Congressional Record*, LVIII (November 19, 1919), 8819.
[5] *New York World*, November 19, 1919.

fore July of 1919 for cotton sold in October, 1918.[6]

Individuals protested against landlords who would not give them itemized statements and equitable settlements, but these attempts failed and further persecution followed. The black tenant farmers' answer was a legitimate alliance of black farmers in Phillips County to end a "vicious system of economic exploitation." [7] These people formed The Organization of the Progressive Farmers' and Household Union of America.[8]

Robert L. Hill founded the Union and often used the title "United States and Foreign Detective" in Union meetings and in signing its stationary. V. E. Powell, a medical doctor, also a founder and examiner of the Union, had printed after his signature on the application forms, "Employed in the U.S. Service." At the top of many circulars mastheads read "Orders of Washington, D.C. The Great Torch of Liberty." [9] Contrary to popular belief at the time, there existed no indication of any other motive in the minds of the leaders of the Union than that of aspiring toward relief from "exploitation" and the acquisition of wealth which the rising price of cotton could bring these farmers by more equitable settlements.[10]

[6] O. A. Rogers, Jr., 143.
[7] White, "Conflict In Arkansas," 234.
[8] This organization henceforth shall be referred to as the Union.
[9] O. A. Rogers, Jr., 146.
[10] *Ibid.*; Chicago *Defender*, February 28, 1920, maintained that the market price of cotton was forty-five cents per pound, but landlords would pay tenant farmers no more than twenty-four cents per pound. The Memphis *Commercial Appeal*, September 29, 1919,

In order to be successful the Union had to have lodges and members. Hill therefore issued a proclamation with the caption "The Negro Business League" which read:

Join the Progressive Farmers' and Household Union of America. O, you laborers of the earth hear the word! The time is at hand that all men, all nations and tongues must receive a just reward! The union wants you to know why it is that the laborers can not control their just earnings which they work for. Some of the leading business merchants and authorities are saying [sic] we are pleading the right cause and are due consideration. There are many of our families suffering because our men are forced to act as children. We also plead that we be recognized as taxpaying citizens. Remember the Holy Word when the Almighty took John up on the mountain and commanded him to look, and asked John what he saw, and John said: "I see all nations and tongues coming up before God." Now, we are a nation and a tongue. Why should we be cut off from fair play? Hear us, O God, hear us! We only ask every Negro man for $1.50 for joining fees; women, 50 cents. Write Box 31, Winchester, Ark., and we will come down and set up a body among you. Get 15 men and 12 women. We will set up together.[11]

As a result of response to this proclamation, blacks established lodges of the Union from April through

stated that cotton prices, different grades included, ranged from twenty-two cents to thirty-four cents a pound.
[11] *New York World*, November 19, 1919. U.S., *Congressional Record*, LVIII (November 19, 1919), 8819.

August, at Elaine, Hoop Spur, Old Town, Ratio, Mellwood, Countiss, and Ferguson. The objective of their
Union remained "to advance the interests of black
people, morally and intellectually, and to make them
better citizens and better farmers." The Union, first
organized in 1919 by Hill at Winchester, Arkansas, had
its articles of incorporation drawn up by Williamson
and Williamson, white attorneys of Monticello, and
filed in legal form. Its constitution contained provisions
for passwords, door words, grips, and signs, all to be
changed every three months to insure secrecy. Those
who violated the Union's secrecy faced either fine or
expulsion, and an expelled member could only be rein-
stated after a ninety-nine-year period. Members in
good standing could not associate with the ostracized
person.[12]

With the stabilization of the Union, various incidents
produced a mounting racial antagonism. The black
sawmill workers of Elaine refused to allow their wives
and daughters to pick cotton or to work for the whites
at any price. Other blacks refused to pick cotton unless
paid their own price, and reports stated that many
refused to work for white farmers at any wages.[13] Edward Ware, secretary of a lodge, refused to sell his cotton for offers varying from twenty-four cents to thirty-
three cents a pound when a fairer market price of
forty-six cents existed. Friction developed between

[12] O. A. Rogers, Jr., 144–45.
[13] Ibid., 144.

Ware and his merchants; finally Ware sought the services of a Helena lawyer. This protest by legal means against the existing economic exploitation further strained interracial relations between Union members and the white community. An atmosphere of tension developed rapidly, and trouble seemed inevitable.

The Union found its strength in numbers and organization. Each member pledged himself to protect the others since the blacks expressed disgust at being expected and forced to act as children. In local meetings members made denunciations and inflammatory speeches against the white planters. At the same time, Union members began to arm themselves for defensive purposes, fully aware of the danger in this course of action. Rumors started to circulate around Elaine to the effect that the blacks were "plotting an uprising" and planning to "slaughter a large number of whites" if a peaceful division of the land could not be obtained.[14]

The firm of Bratton, Bratton, and Casey, attorneys of Little Rock, set up a branch office in Helena. At Hill's suggestion, the youngest Bratton entered into contracts with the black people to enforce a settlement for them and to sue for all moneys due them in the past.[15] Each of sixty-eight blacks agreed to pay the firm twenty-five dollars in cash and a percentage of the money collected from the landowners. The blacks met

[14] *Ibid.,* 146–47.
[15] *New York World,* November 19, 1919. U.S., *Congressional Record,* LVIII (November 19, 1919), 8819.

secretly to discuss their plight and to collect the lawyers'
fees. Some reportedly wanted to go before the grand
jury to charge their landlords with peonage.[16]

Hill attended a meeting of the Union at Hoop Spur
on Friday night, September 26. At a large and quite
enthusiastic gathering, Hill spoke "very strongly"
against the whites and reiterated that the black race's
salvation lay in organization. Furthermore, Hill insisted that all meetings be well guarded and that "no
whites should be allowed to molest" the members or the
meetings.[17]

The Union held another meeting at Hoop Spur on
the night of October 1, but Hill did not appear. The
church, filled to capacity, had two rings of guards hold-
ing rifles and shotguns, posted outside it. The guards,
seeing the headlight of an approaching automobile,
withdrew to the brush to let it pass. At a small stream
near the church the automobile stopped, and the guards
silently drew near. A white man stood near the car and
said, "Going coon hunting, boys?" The guards made no
reply and withdrew. Someone fired a shot. Shots then
became numerous and the meeting erupted. Blacks
leaped through windows of the church and hurriedly

16 O. A. Rogers, Jr., 144. On p. 145, Rogers states that, "At the
time of the riot the Union seemed to have been adhering to the
constitution. Plans were being made to buy some farm land at
Mellwood, and the members had planned to build a 'temple' at
Winchester."
17 *New York World*, November 19, 1919. U.S., *Congressional Record*, LVIII (November 19, 1919), 8820.

moved through other exits to all parts of the county.[18]

The men in the car turned out to be Special Agent W. A. Adkins of the Missouri Pacific Railroad, Sheriff's Deputy Charles Pratt, and a black "trusty." Early on the night of October 1, a message from law officers in Elaine stated that a notorious bootlegger known only as "Clem" had "gone on a rampage," and threatened to kill his wife. Sheriff Kitchen sent a posse composed of Special Agent Adkins, Sheriff's Deputy Pratt, and the black "trusty" to arrest Clem and other disorderly citizens.[19] The posse claimed that their car broke down, and that the blacks fired upon them first. Adkins died instantly, and Pratt received a bullet through his knee. The black "trusty" escaped unhurt and reported the shooting by telephone to the citizens of Helena. He told of a vicious attack and stated that there was still fighting going on. Pratt, in the meantime, crawled to the railroad, flagged a freight train, and upon arriving at the station, telephoned an account of the shooting to Sheriff Kitchen in Helena. In a later report the blacks claimed that Adkins and Pratt fired upon them with the intention of breaking up their meeting.[20]

A white man named Monroe stopped at the scene an

[18] *New York World*, November 19, 1919. Accounts vary as to exactly which group fired the first shot.
[19] Memphis *Commercial Appeal*, October 2, 1919, 1–2. Waskow, 124–28.
[20] White, 233–34; O. A. Rogers, Jr., 147; New York *World*, November 19, 1919. U.S. *Congressional Record*, LVIII (November 19, 1919), 8820.

hour later, about 1:30 A.M., to view the automobile and the dead man. Shot at and wounded twice, he still managed to "crank" his Ford and get through to Elaine, two miles away, and telephone the sheriff. Men of Elaine assembled in the streets before daylight. The sheriff issued guns, and meetings by leading men of both races prepared methods of keeping the peace. The governor, Charles H. Brough, advised of conditions, led a posse of men, all made deputy sheriffs, to Hoop Spur. The first men to arrive upon the scene came from the American Legion camp composed of newly returned war veterans.[21]

By early Thursday morning, October 2, word had already circulated among the blacks around Elaine that "the whites were going to kill all black people." [22] Many crossed the railroad tracks to hide from the posse in the canebrakes.[23] News of Adkins's death precipitated a state of serious racial antagonism. White men, pouring into the area from all parts of Arkansas, Mississippi, and Tennessee, disarmed and arrested black people. The confiscated guns then were given to the whites, who rapidly descended upon the little town of Helena. Those blacks who escaped arrest "were hunted down like animals." [24]

---

[21] *New York World*, November 19, 1919. U.S., *Congressional Record*, LVIII (November 19, 1919), 8820.
[22] O. A. Rogers, Jr., 148.
[23] J. W. Butts and Dorothy James, "The Underlying Causes of the Elaine Riot of 1919," *Arkansas Historical Quarterly*, XX (1961), 101.
[24] White, 234.

Early reports said that 1,000 to 1,500 blacks had assembled and attacked the white residents using high-powered rifles. A Helena telephone operator, between screams, told an official in Elaine that fighting raged in the streets; and other messages called for additional enforcements, guns, and ammunition, and asked the sheriff to request the governor to send troops from Camp Pike and Little Rock.[25] At one period of the fighting Chief Deputy J. R. Dalsell, in charge of the posse at Elaine, telephoned that he must have help; that his force was greatly outnumbered; and that firing had become general. Special trains rushed to and from Elaine and Helena carrying wounded men, women, and children.[26]

When a posse of white men arrived at Elaine from Helena, they began to search and ransack the homes of black people, arresting men and women indiscriminately. Exchanges of gunfire occurred, and men fell dead on both sides. As the situation got worse, Sheriff Kitchen requested Governor Brough to send troops from Camp Pike. The governor granted the request, and troops, under the command of Colonel I. C. Jenks, Third Division, immediately on arrival, ordered a battalion, under the command of Major N. E. Callen, to deploy and start a search of the canebrakes to the west of Elaine. Another detachment went to Mellwood, and others went to several small settlements nearby. Colonel Jenks dispatched another company of soldiers to Helena

[25] Memphis *Commercial Appeal*, October 2, 1919, 2.
[26] *Ibid.*

late on the afternoon of October 2, on a special train of the Missouri Pacific Railroad to stop any trouble that might start there.[27] Five hundred soldiers, armed with twelve machine guns and other weapons, rode to Elaine, then under martial law, and they "anxiously" joined their white comrades in the fighting against the blacks. They rounded up all black people, arrested them and placed them in a stockade as the troops and posses combed the area around Elaine for a radius of fifty miles. In some spots shooting so frequently erupted that even Governor Brough had to dodge bullets while following troops into the canebrakes.[28]

Later reports stated that some blacks had been driven from Elaine, but that fighting still progressed one mile to the north, where the "outlaws" rallied and supposedly received reinforcements. After several encounters shooting finally died down late in the evening of October 2, and straggling posses began to dribble into Helena. They brought with them all kinds of stories, but through them all ran the strong suspicion that the rioting appeared to have been caused by "propaganda" furnished by white men. Whether these white men could be connected with the gang of bootleggers that operated in the canebrakes near Elaine and Lambrook remained a puzzle. Most whites felt rather cer-

[27] *Ibid.*, October 3, 1919, 1; O. A. Rogers, Jr., 148.
[28] O. A. Rogers, Jr., 148. According to Butts and James, 95, there was "no fighting itself" in Elaine at any time, "all of the fighting took place at Hoop Spur, or in the woods around Elaine."

tain, however, that an organization of blacks antagonistic to the whites existed in the southern part of the county.[29] The troops arrested more blacks and herded them into the stockade. They refused the captives communication with relatives, friends, or attorneys. Although a black person might be able to prove his innocence, he could not be released until a white person vouched for him. In many instances this support did not take place until the black person agreed to work for his white patron for a period of time and for wages scaled by the employer.[30] O. S. Bratton, lawyer for the Union, met with a group of blacks at Ratio to plan court strategy for forcing back settlements on cotton sales. A posse broke up this conference, and arrested Bratton and approximately seventy blacks. Bratton and fifteen blacks arrived in Helena under heavy guard. Presumably, Bratton led the blacks who had opposed the officers and citizens. The jail at Elaine "was very strongly guarded," but feelings boiled "above fever heat." Jailed for thirty-one days without a hearing on a charge of "barratry," or fomenting legal action, Bratton finally secured his freedom by posting bond.[31] According to Bratton's father, U.S. Bratton, his son had nothing to do either with the murder or with inciting to riot, since

[29] Memphis *Commercial Appeal*, October 2, 1919, 2. "An unconfirmed report persisted stating that blacks in the Elaine section had received letters from 'French girls' telling them to rise against the whites and secure their rights."

[30] White, 234.

[31] *Ibid.*, 233–34; Memphis *Commercial Appeal*, October 2, 1919, 1.

his family never advocated social equality and always advised blacks to obey the law.[32]

On Thursday afternoon, October 3, the posses found Elihu Johnson, black, and his three brothers hiding south of Elaine, all heavily armed. Johnson, a Helena dentist, appeared to be well-to-do. The deputies disarmed the four and put them in the back seat of an automobile, and the deputies sat up front. They then started for Helena. At a gasoline stop two of the white men got out. One of the Johnson brothers reportedly leaned forward, seized Orley R. Lilly's revolver, and killed him. The other white men killed the four Johnson brothers on the spot.[33]

Later that evening somebody shot James A. Tappan, white, from ambush, and a soldier, Corporal Earls, died of gunshot wounds. Soon after these deaths the posses and soldiers had most of the armed blacks penned down in the canebrakes. Of the 700 members of the Union in Phillips County, more than 400 hid in the canebrakes. Before being flushed out more than twenty blacks had been killed. The Helena jail and courthouse overflowed with prisoners. Three big army trucks supposedly carried the captured rifles and shotguns.[34] In West Helena, Henry Sloan, black, found himself in jail on a charge of making "incendiary speeches" in the black section of that city. Whites of West Helena said that "the Negroes

[32] Memphis *Commercial Appeal*, October 3, 1919, 2.
[33] *New York World*, November 19, 1919; U.S., *Congressional Record*, LVIII (November 19, 1919), 8820.
[34] *Ibid.*

of that city have conducted themselves most commendably during the disturbances of the past three days." [35] Meanwhile, someone reportedly saw Hill near his farm. This appeared to be the last time anyone saw Hill in Arkansas, and he remained the only prominent member of the Union unaccounted for. He had withdrawn $12,000 from the local bank.[36]

On the night of October 3, Governor Brough appointed a committee of seven prominent citizens with full authority to conduct a complete investigation. According to the statement of E. M. Allen, a founder of Elaine and a member of the committee, the real underlying causes of this "insurrection" stand out as "avarice and greed." An abstract of Allen's report showed that the trouble with the blacks in Phillips County happened not to be a racial riot, but a "deliberately planned insurrection" of the blacks against the whites directed by an organization known as the Progressive Farmers' and Household Union of America. Its founder, Robert L. Hill, of Winchester, Arkansas, saw in it "an opportunity of making easy money." According to Allen's report, Hill told the blacks that he had become "an agent" of the United States government in defense of the blacks against the whites; that it appeared necessary for all members of the Union to arm themselves; and that all lodge meetings must maintain an outer guard.

---

[35] Memphis *Commercial Appeal*, October 4, 1919, 2.
[36] *New York World*, November 19, 1919; U.S., *Congressional Record*, LVIII (November 19, 1919), 8820.

Furthermore, Hill presumably told the blacks that the government planned to construct at Winchester three warehouses where "arms, ammunition, and trained soldiers would be ready for instant use." [37]

Allen reportedly found that Hill had many "schemes" for obtaining money from the lodge members. Hill sold certificates, those for registration costing fifty cents and those for admission to the lodge in Winchester costing five dollars. Shares for a building to be constructed at Winchester went on sale at ten dollars each, and all members purchasing five or more shares supposedly had their names engraved therein. Hill made some members "private and foreign detectives" and sold them nickel-plated stars and handcuffs for fifty dollars each. He procured government maps of land in the Elaine area which he said could be purchased for $200, the purchase price to be raised and paid to Hill in cash. Certain blacks, after receiving descriptions of the land, supposedly designated which parts of the various farms, then under cultivation, they wished to obtain after "the whites had been driven off." Allen also found that black soldiers at Elaine sold their discharge papers for sums of fifty to one hundred dollars on a theory that these discharges entitled the holder to forty acres of government land. Furthermore, according to Allen, Hill so planned his campaign that "any black, possessing from fifty cents to fifty dollars, was given the

[37] Butts and James, 99; Seligmann, "Race Hatred," 541.

opportunity to invest in something connected with the Union." [38]

The report of the committee of seven said in effect that the shooting at Hoop Spur nipped a "mature plan of insurrection" by members of the Union against the white population of Phillips County. Taking place on October 6, 1919, the alleged uprising supposedly marked twenty-one white men for death. Many persons failed to believe the "official report" of the committee because it had been composed by local white leaders, including two plantation owners. The report alleged that the Union's literature demanded "social equality and resistance to injustice," that the blacks were heavily armed with a large quantity of guns and ammunition, that they "fought back" and killed five white men, and that many blacks confessed to having been a part of a "well-laid plan to kill twenty-one white planters." After the accused had been granted proper legal counsel the principal confessions changed noticeably, and most denied charges of being parties to an insurrection. In the final analysis, the issuance of the committee's report "served only to aggravate an already bad situation." [39]

By the last of the week those blacks not in jail went back to work picking cotton or spending seed money. The "best" lawyers in Phillips County, stated the *New*

[38] Butts and James, 100.
[39] O. A. Rogers, Jr., 148–49.

*York World*, received appointments from Judge M. M. Jackson to defend the blacks accused of murder. Colonel George W. Murphy, white, of Little Rock, former attorney general of Arkansas, and Scipio Jones, black, prominent lawyer of Little Rock, represented the accused men.[40] According to Arkansas law each party to a conspiracy is guilty of all crimes emanating from the conspiracy; therefore, all the accused blacks could have been indicted for first degree murder, but the court "earnestly" tried to administer a "fairer" justice. Assuredly the lawyers prepared the cases with great care before court convened. The all-white jury did not delay in finding verdicts, some after only from two to ten minutes of deliberation.[41] The judge did not allow witnesses for the defense to testify. The defense did not ask for a change of venue, and the trials started one month after the incident while ill feelings remained intense. The first six defendants appeared. The judge and jury jointly indicted them, tried them, and found them guilty in exactly seven minutes. The jury sentenced the six men to electrocution on December 27, 1919, for first degree murder.[42] Of the fifty blacks found guilty of second degree murder, ten received twenty-one-year terms in the state penitentiary. Eleven

[40] *New York World*, November 19, 1919; U.S., *Congressional Record*, LVIII (November 19, 1919), 8820; Chicago *Defender*, December 27, 1919.
[41] *New York World*, November 19, 1919; U.S., *Congressional Record*, LVIII (November 19, 1919), 8820.
[42] White, "Conflict in Arkansas," 234.

blacks got one-year terms for night-riding, which is a
felony in Arkansas. The judge bound thirty persons
over to the next grand jury and released them on
bond.[43]

The twelve condemned men were Edward Ware,
Albert Giles, Joseph Fox, John Martin, Alf Banks, Jr.,
William Wordlow, Frank Moore, Edward Hicks, J. E.
Knox, Edward Coleman, Paul Hall, and Frank Hicks.
Their petition for a writ of certiorari to the Supreme
Court of the State of Arkansas was denied on October
11, 1920, and they were executed.[44] Although authori-
ties arrested Robert L. Hill in Kansas, Governor Henry
Allen would not extradite him to Arkansas because he
believed Hill would not receive a fair trial.[45] With the
first and second degree murder trials a farce, "the sys-
tem" remained intact, and things got back to normal in
Phillips County, Arkansas.

[43] New York World, November 19, 1919; U.S., Congressional Record, LVIII (November 19, 1919), 8820.
[44] Frank Moore et. al., Petitioners v. Arkansas, 254 U.S. 630
(1920). Vol. XLI in The Supreme Court Reporter (St. Paul: West
Publishing Company, 1922), 7–8.
[45] Chicago Defender, January 1, 1920; Butts and James, 104.

# CHAPTER IV

# The Tulsa Riot

The distorted and exaggerated report of a white woman employed as an elevator operator triggered a racial outbreak in the crime-racked city of Tulsa, Oklahoma, in 1921. Before the riot occurred a violent atmosphere had prevailed in that Oklahoma boom town, which had become a haven of crime and corruption. Insurance companies even refused to insure the stocks of local merchants because of the high risk of theft. A number of companies canceled all policies covering automobiles because so many had been stolen. In July, 1920, a mob "liberated" Roy Belton, a white man accused of murdering a cab driver, from the county jail and summarily lynched him. According to many prominent Tulsans, "local policemen directed traffic at the scene of the lynching," in an effort to allow every person present "an equal chance to view the event." Criminal acts became the order of the day, and as a result of these conditions hardly a soul in Tulsa, black or white, had very much respect for the law.[1]

No riot ever engulfed a city with less warning or found the local authorities less prepared with corrective measures. It appeared to be a "spontaneous flare-up" based upon prejudices, suspicions, and rumors.[2] Un-

[1] Walter F. White, "The Eruption of Tulsa," *Nation*, CXII (June 29, 1921), 909.
[2] "The Tulsa Race Riots," *Independent and Weekly Review*, CV (June 18, 1921), 646.

scrupulous Tulsa journalists published reports of an incident which helped start the worst racial clash since that of East St. Louis, Illinois, in 1917. The Tulsa *Tribune* reported that a white girl had been "assaulted" by a black man when, in fact, the black man, a bootblack by trade, accidentally stepped on the elevator girl's foot. She slapped him and he, in retaliation, grabbed her and then fled.[3]

Thus on Monday, May 30, 1921, Sarah Page, operating an elevator in the Drexel Building, told police that Dick Rowland, nineteen, attempted to "criminally assault her." Her second story reported that the young man grabbed her arm as he entered the elevator. A few hours later police found that he had stepped, accidentally, on her foot. Apparently the citizens of Tulsa never thought that a man attempting criminal assault would have chosen any place other than an open elevator in a public building. On May 31, the Tulsa *Tribune*, one of two dailies, printed this story of alleged assault. Around four o'clock that afternoon Commissioner of Police J. M. Adkinson reported to Sheriff McCullough that whites talked about lynching Rowland that night. Also, Chief of Police John A. Gustafson, Captain Wilkerson of the police department, Edwin F. Barnett, managing editor of the Tulsa *Tribune*, and many other citizens told of the spread of lynching rumors. Rowland was thereupon apprehended and taken into cus-

[3] White, "Eruption of Tulsa," 909–10.

tody. After rioting broke out a little later, he was removed from the jail by the police, and his whereabouts
were not made public.[4]

In the meantime the rumors of the threatened lynching penetrated throughout the black district, where
15,000 black Tulsans lived. Recalling how a white man
had been taken from the county jail and lynched just a
few months earlier, they feared that Rowland would
be in danger because he was in the same jail and was
black. A group of black men telephoned the sheriff and
offered to aid in protecting the jail from attack. The
sheriff told them that they would be contacted if
needed. Around nine o'clock that night a crowd of
some four hundred white men gathered around Rowland's place of incarceration. Approximately fifteen
minutes later a rumor reached "Little Africa" that the
mob had "stormed" the jail. Twenty-five black men
immediately marched to the scene, but they found the
rumor to be false. The sheriff talked with them, urged
them to return home, and assured them that no harm
would come to Rowland. They left, but upon hearing
more gross rumors of "whites storming the jail," returned seventy-five strong, all bearing arms. The sheriff
again persuaded them to leave, but as they were departing a white man tried to take a gun away from one of
the blacks. A shot rang out, and in Sheriff McCullough's

---

[4] *Ibid.*; *New York Times*, June 2, 1921, 1, stated that Dick Rowland was arrested and charged with assault; Memphis *Commercial
Appeal*, June 3, 1921.

words, "all hell broke loose." There were dozens of shots from both sides and twelve men fell dead—two black and ten white. The fighting continued until midnight and the greatly outnumbered black men had to retreat to "Little Africa." [5] When the whites found that they were inadequately supplied with weapons, they looted hardware and sporting goods' stores to secure rifles, revolvers, and ammunition. Many then formed "automobile parties" and rode unchallenged through the streets with guns in hand. [6]

Soon after the outbreaks at the courthouse and jail the authorities realized their inability to control the fighting with police alone. A call went out to Governor James B. A. Robertson for troops. The Governor promptly directed Adjutant General Charles F. Barnett to take any steps necessary to handle the trouble. Barnett ordered three companies of State Militia to Tulsa and sent instructions to commanding officers in several nearby towns to be prepared to rush men and equipment to Tulsa on immediate notice. Local Guardsmen were stationed around the courthouse and jail to prevent a mob from breaking through. [7]

By dawn of Wednesday, June 1, the whites were in command of the situation. For three consecutive days they had warned the blacks on the front page of a Tulsa newspaper that on June 1 the black population would

[5] White, "Eruption of Tulsa," 910.
[6] "The Tulsa Riots," 646.
[7] New York Times, June 2, 1921, 2.

be cleared out. This threat was repeated on "unsigned cards" pasted on the doors of black-owned houses.[8]

Neither the sheriff nor the police department took any effective steps to put a stop to the lawlessness of either group. As the morning progressed the rioting took on a new and more sinister phase. Five hundred white men and one thousand black men fired at each other across the railroad tracks. Police learned that the bodies of from six to ten blacks could be seen lying in an area described as "no man's land." The police later received a report that three railway switchmen and a brakeman had died in the shooting. The trainmen were killed because they refused to permit members of the opposing groups to ride on a switch engine passing between the lines. The engineer escaped the gunfire.[9] The whites, no longer content with a negative victory, planned to carry the war into the opponents' territory.

They decided to invade "Niggertown" and systematically wipe it out. Presumably they intended to commit arson rather than outright murder. Every building, therefore, would be put to the torch, including a church, a new school, two newspaper offices, and several three-story structures. With their plans and targets set, more than ten thousand whites, equipped with pistols, rifles, machine guns, and gasoline bombs, massed for the invasion. From sixty to eighty automobiles filled with armed white men formed a circle

[8] "The Tulsa Riots," 646.
[9] *New York Times*, June 2, 1921, 2.

around the black section. The white men also used eight airplanes to spy on the movements of the blacks and, according to some reports, used the planes to bomb the black section.[10] The only thing absent from this "modern Christian warfare" was poison gas. By mid-morning the invasion was in full swing. The black men and women fought valiantly but vainly to defend their homes, but the odds were too great. According to on-lookers, men in uniform—home guards or ex-service-men, or both—carried cans of oil and gasoline into "Niggertown" and, after first looting the homes, set them on fire. Many later told tales of horror committed, not by blacks, but by whites. One story was that of an aged black couple killed while saying their prayers before retiring in their little home on Greenwood Avenue. A mob broke into the house, shot both of the old people in the backs of their heads, pillaged the house, and then set it on fire. Other reports told of raiders firing into crowds of fleeing blacks.[11]

Dr. A. C. Jackson, a black physician, became a victim of the rioting. He had been described by the famous Mayo brothers as "the most able Negro surgeon in America." Both whites and blacks alike respected him. A mob attacked Dr. Jackson's home, and he fought to protect it, his family, and himself. An officer of the home guards came up and assured him that, if he would surrender, he would be protected. In good faith, Dr.

[10] *Ibid.*; White, "Eruption of Tulsa," 910.
[11] "Blood and Oil," *Survey*, XLVI (June 11, 1921), 369.

Jackson surrendered, and the officer sent him under guard to Convention Hall, where black people were being placed for protection. On the way to the hall, a white man shot and killed Dr. Jackson in cold blood. The officer who had assured him of protection commented that, "Dr. Jackson was an able, clean-cut man. He did only what any red-blooded man would have done under similar circumstances in defending his home. Dr. Jackson was murdered by white ruffians." [12]

The heaviest fighting occurred in the northern section, where hundreds of blacks concentrated in a valley. Fifty or more barricaded themselves in a church. The whites launched several massed attacks against the church, but each time the attackers fell back under fire from the black defenders. Finally, a torch applied to the church set it ablaze, and the occupants began to pour out, shooting as they ran. Several blacks were killed. Apparently, the blacks had expected trouble and were prepared for the whites. Explosions of boxes of shells resounded in almost every second house that burned, and the police said that the International Workers of the World and other "malcontents" had stirred up animosity between the races for months prior to the riot. [13]

When darkness came much additional damage resulted to the black district in prolonged attempts "to smoke the demon out." The fire department attempted but did not succeed in stopping the fires from spreading.

[12] White, "Eruption of Tulsa," 910.
[13] *New York Times*, June 2, 1921, 2.

The entire black belt became a smoldering heap of blackened ruins. Hardly a shanty, house, or building was left standing throughout the area. Domestic animals wandering among the wreckage gave the only signs of life in the desolated territory. The area of destruction extended from the Frisco Railway Company tracks to Sand Pipe Hill. Looting by lawless elements continued sporadically.[14] Ironically, when blacks sought to liberate themselves from the "black ghetto" before it burned, the whites denounced them for their insolence in intruding upon the white man's kingdom and lowering the property values. Meanwhile whites cursed blacks because their environment bred contagious diseases, immorality, and vice. If criminals born in this animal-like sanctuary chanced to come out, whites would lynch them. Furthermore, threats of lynching or attack were made against innocent black people reared under these same conditions.[15]

On Thursday morning, June 2, thousands of black families, unable to get far from the scene of terror, camped on the hills surrounding the city. The Humane Society, the local chapter of the Red Cross, and other social agencies immediately began working to provide the blacks with food, clothing, and water. Churches, schools, public buildings, and private homes later became temporary homes for many people. The police arrested a few looters, but within twenty-four hours

[14] *Ibid.*, 1.
[15] "Tulsa," *Nation*, CXII (June 15, 1921), 839.

tensions became so relieved that two hundred and fifty of five hundred Guardsmen returned to their home stations. Martial law was declared in the city of Tulsa and in Tulsa County. Ordinances, promulgated by military authorities, established a seven o'clock curfew. No person, white or black, could go out of his lodging after that hour without credentials. The remaining state Guardsmen patrolled the streets of the business and railroad districts. Police in automobiles moved through the city to break up suspicious gatherings. All blacks that could not be accommodated in temporary homes had to be placed in detention camps. The largest of these camps, the baseball park, housed six thousand blacks.[16]

The mayor withdrew all special police commissions because some of these special officers turned out to be ringleaders in the shooting. Reports indicated that the exact number of casualties will never be known. Originally, the press estimated one hundred dead, but the number buried by local undertakers and cited by city officials totaled 10 whites and 21 blacks. Obviously, the city officials wanted to keep the number as low as possible, but unofficial reports in Tulsa put the number much higher. Fifty whites and between 150 to 200 blacks would appear to be a more accurate count of the number of deaths.[17] According to O. T. Johnson, commandant of the Tulsa Citadel of the Salvation Army, 57 black gravediggers dug more than 120 graves

[16] "Blood and Oil," 370; *New York Times*, June 2, 1921, 1.
[17] White, "Eruption of Tulsa," 910.

and placed 1 black body in each, using no coffins. They simply dumped the bodies into the holes and covered them with dirt. Many persons incinerated in the burning houses of the black district remained unaccounted for. An eyewitness related that of 5 black men trapped in a burning house, 4 burned to death. The fifth man, trying to escape the flames, emerged from the house and died in the ensuing gun battle. His body was thrown back into the fire. According to rumor, two trucks loaded with dead blacks dumped them into the Arkansas River, but this rumor could not be confirmed.[18]

John A. Gustafson, police chief of Tulsa, lost his job after being found guilty by a jury of neglect and conspiracy in connection with the riot. Mrs. Katherine Van Leuven, assistant attorney general, charged in her prosecution that the chief could have disarmed those who first gathered at the courthouse and prevented the riot. She then "threw the fat in the fire" by stating that after the armed blacks had begun shooting and "killed a white man," those who armed themselves for the obvious purpose of "protecting their lives and property violated no law." [19] A reporter for the *Defender* reacted in his article to Mrs. Van Leuven's statement in the following manner:

> Certainly the white mob violated no law. Who dares to say that they did not have a perfect right to shoot

18 *Ibid.*
19 Chicago *Defender*, July 30, 1921.

down every innocent black man, woman or child, and burn and pillage whole sections where black men lived? If a white ruffian shoots another white ruffian the rest of the white race immediately attempts to slaughter scores of other white people, do they not? Yes—they do not. These so-called Americans are so humane, so considerate, so just it really is a pleasure to live in their midst. What effect can such a statement as the one by Mrs. Van Leuven have on semi-barbarians than to encourage further violence? We are happy to note, of course, that Tulsa is trying to atone for her misdeeds, but let her come not with an olive branch in one hand and a dagger in the other hidden behind the back.[20]

The loss in property ran over $1,500,000, families were rendered homeless, and the business community appeared completely demoralized; but the black citizenry of Tulsa pushed resolutely forward toward reconstruction of their lost fortunes. City authorities and bankers added to the plight of the blacks by refusing to grant them loans or aid. In light of this situation the black people organized to rebuild their community under the leadership of O. W. Gurley, president of the East End Welfare Board; D. D. Hooker, chairman of the relief committee; John Tyler Smith, treasurer; and Mrs. D. L. Bush, secretary. The group employed attorneys I. E. Sadler, W. P. Brown, R. Emmit Stewart, and Elisha Scott to aid, advise, and protect their legal interest.[21]

[20] *Ibid.*
[21] *Ibid.*, July 23, 1921; Thompson and Hughes (eds.), 398–99; "Blood and Oil," 369.

The National Association for the Advancement of Colored People, in addition to starting a relief fund for the homeless, collected additional evidence of racial discrimination in Oklahoma. It received reports, said James Weldon Johnson, secretary of the Association, that peonage generally prevailed in some parts of the state, and that robbery of black tenants, burning of homes, and brutalities of every description became common, especially after the fall in the price of cotton and the subsequent unemployment of many black workers.[22] But there appeared a lesson in the outrages of Tulsa for all Americans who fatuously believed that black people would always be "the meek submissive creatures that circumstances [had] forced them to be during the past three hundred years." Although Dick Rowland was only an ordinary bootblack, when his life became threatened by a white mob, nearly all the 15,000 blacks of Tulsa fought to protect him.[23]

What were the causes of the racial riot that occurred in Tulsa? Many authors have offered reasons and explanations which are worthy of consideration. According to one writer, the black people in Oklahoma shared in the overnight prosperity that came to many whites, and some blacks became powerful and wealthy. This fact caused a bitter resentment in the ranks of the lower-class whites, who felt that these blacks, members of an "inferior" race, overstepped their bounds by

22 "Blood and Oil," 370.
23 White, "Eruption of Tulsa," 910.

achieving greater economic prosperity than those members of the "divinely ordered superior race." At least three black persons in Oklahoma held fortunes of $1,000,000 each, and many others amassed fortunes ranging from $25,000 to $500,000.[24] In one instance a black man owned and operated a printing house with $25,000 worth of printing machinery in it. The leader of the mob that set fire to and destroyed the establishment was a white linotype operator employed for years by the black owner at forty-eight dollars per week. The worker met his death in the attack. The whites who populated Oklahoma came primarily from other states, many being former residents of Mississippi, Georgia, Alabama, Tennessee, Texas, and other southern states. These pioneers had brought with them their anti-black prejudices.[25]

Another cause advanced by White stated that the blacks of Tulsa affronted the whites with "radical" action. He found that black people uncompromisingly denounced "Jim Crow" cars, lynching, and peonage. In short, they asked that federal constitutional guaranties be given to all regardless of color. The blacks of Tulsa and other Oklahoma cities dared to be men and women. Those whites who sought to maintain "the old white group control" could not stomach seeing blacks liberating themselves from the old system.[26]

[24] *Ibid.*, 909.
[25] *Ibid.*
[26] *Ibid.*

The lack of law enforcement contributed to the rioting in Tulsa, and corrupt political conditions added to the problem. A vice ring controlled the city and allowed open operation of houses of prostitution, gambling parlors, illegal whiskey sales, and bank and store robberies.[27] Only a slight possibility existed of the arrest of criminals and even less of their conviction. For fourteen years, Tulsa groaned under the absolute control of hoodlums. Most of the upstanding citizenry interested themselves only in making money and departing the city. They took little or no interest in the election of city and county officials. The community leaders left the situation to those in whose interest it was to elect officials who would protect them and their crooked operations. Things were so bad in April, 1921, that the state legislature assigned two additional judges to Tulsa County to aid the two judges already sitting to clear the swollen dockets. These judges found more than 6,000 cases awaiting trial. Notably, in a county with a population of just over 100,000 persons, "six out of every one hundred persons" lived under indictment for some crime with trial unlikely in any of the cases.[28]

Comstock believes that it was in the sordid and neglected "Niggertown" that the hoodlums found their best sanctuary. A "cesspool" of crime prevailed. In the brothels low whites mixed with low blacks. Narcotic

[27] Amy Comstock, " 'Over There,' Another View of the Tulsa Riots," *Survey*, XLVI (July 2, 1921), 460.
[28] *Ibid.*; White, "Eruption of Tulsa," 909.

vendors and consumers thrived there. Criminals plotted
crimes and hid loot there. City administrators kept an
eagle's eye upon the "uptown traffic regulations," but
left the black section to police itself. For months prior
to the riot, the "bad niggers, the silk-shirted parasites of
society," collected guns and ammunitions. Tulsa, therefore, lived on a Vesuvius that could "vomit fire" at any
time. Officials admitted that they knew of the riot situation but hoped it would pass away because "the argo-
nauts were all too busy panning gold to care." [29]

The hurried construction of Tulsa neglected "Niggertown." Coming into Tulsa via the Santa Fe Railway one would have seen numerous "impoverished
shanties" with "out-houses standing on stilts," and yards
in "conspicuous disorder." Water mains, for fire prevention only, ran through the section, and no sewers
existed.[30]

Along with whites, many blacks from southern states
bought small parcels of oil land in Oklahoma from the
Indians. Since they proved good investments, some five
hundred black owners resisted all offers, often accompanied by threats, to sell these lands for less than
their actual value. Every increase in the price of oil
produced more bitterness and strife. When a depression
descended upon the labor market, white employers
thought they had the upper hand and demanded that
black employees sell out or quit. Petty persecutions be-

[29] Page 460.
[30] *Ibid.*

came common, but no widespread violence had occurred in the past years.[31] Various factors, therefore,
led to the 1921 rioting in Tulsa, and, according to
Comstock, Tulsa "repented" for her sins. In an effort to
eliminate further riots or strained racial relations, Tulsa
hoped to put into action a social program consisting of
a city plan for future construction, a more efficient
police department, commercial and industrial education, recreational facilities, and rehabilitation for drug
addicts.[32]

But had Tulsa really determined to treat and to heal
her racially sore wounds? It is hard to say, when just
two months after the devastating riot city officials permitted Saleb A. Ridley, an Atlanta, Georgia, minister,
to advance, as the reporter put it, the "aims and purposes" of the Ku Klux Klan from the platform of Convention Hall, recently used to house respectable Tulsans
from murderous attacks by "policemen, guardsmen,
and government-owned aircraft." [33] "A white man is a
white man," shouted Ridley, "whether he lives in New
Jersey, Indiana, Kansas, Illinois, Oklahoma, or Georgia.
And a white man's job is to see that civilization comes
under the dominance of no inferior race so long as he
lives." The impassioned address was not interrupted as
the large audience remained quiet and attentive. Apparently, the meeting received the approval of several

[31] "Blood and Oil," 369.
[32] Comstock, 460.
[33] Chicago *Defender*, August 20, 1921.

city officials, for they postponed other duties to hear
the speech.

Ridley declared himself to be an imperial officer in
the Klan and insisted that he was not a paid lecturer for
the organization, but "spent his vacation 'between Sun-
days' speaking for it." Local officials advised Ridley
to avoid reference in his speech to the riot, supposedly
because of the shameful condition of the city of Tulsa.
The Klan obviously sought to strengthen its membership in Oklahoma, since Ridley described the state
as "fertile ground" for the establishment of a "perma-
nent auxilliary," and since several members of the Tulsa
police department expressed their intention of joining
the Klan.[34] As it turned out, Oklahoma became a
"boomer state" for the Klan in the 1920's. By the end
of 1921 more Klansmen were in the Sooner State than
"there had been in the whole Invisible Empire six
months before." [35] There was not a particle of evidence
to connect the Klan with the riot, but it appeared likely
that the brief, devastating racial war gave some impetus
to the Klan's growth in Tulsa.[36]

White Tulsans faced an appalling dilemma. Should
they continue their racist policy of domination over a
so-called inferior race or should they seek to work with

[34] *Ibid.*; see app. D.
[35] David M. Chalmers, *Hooded Americanism: The History of the
Ku Klux Klan* (Chicago: Quadrangle Books, 1968), 49.
[36] Charles C. Alexander, *The Ku Klux Klan in the Southwest*
(Lexington: University of Kentucky Press, 1965), 44; Kenneth T.
Jackson, *The Ku Klux Klan in the City, 1915–1930* (New York:
Oxford University Press, 1967), 85.

the blacks to build a greater Tulsa? A few whites chose
to exercise man's innate goodness by helping the blacks
to recover their lost gains, but most chose to adhere to
man's depraved nature by insisting that "America is
and shall forever remain a white man's country."

# CHAPTER V

# The Chicago Riot

The Chicago riot of 1919 lasted for four days, from July 27 to August 1, and brought death to thirty-six persons. This concentration of violence was no spontaneous combustion, for in the preceeding two years whites had murdered twenty-seven blacks because they dared move from their segregated blocks into white neighborhoods.[1] Typically, the precipitating incident was a small-scale struggle between white and black civilians—often in a public place, such as a beach or in an area of uncertain racial boundaries. Within a few hours the riot would ramble into full swing and continue intermittently with decreasing intensity for a number of days. Whites would invade black areas, and very often the riot spread to the central business district, where the white population outnumbered the blacks. Much of the violence took place on "main thoroughfares and at transfer points," as blacks sought to return to their homes for some sort of refuge. Symbolically, the riot expressed elements of the white community's impulse to "kick the Negro back into his place." [2]

Despite the wide areas engulfed by the riot and the

---

[1] Frederick L. Allen, *Only Yesterday* (New York: Harper and Brothers, 1931), 63; Mark Sullivan, *Our Times: The United States, 1900–1925*. Vol. VI (New York: Charles Scribner's Sons, 1935), 178–79; Thompson and Hughes, (eds.), 400.

[2] The National Commission On the Causes And Prevention Of Violence, 396.

number of casualties inflicted, the whites limited themselves to very small groups, or "nuclei of activists," often encouraged by "vocal bystanders" to take the initiative. The blacks fought back in time, but they seldom invaded white areas. According to available documentation, the whites mainly armed themselves with "bricks and blunt sticks, and also fought with their fists." A limited number of handguns and rifles appeared. On occasion, blacks became better armed because they had more guns and knives. This riot had many incidents of "direct, personal, and brutal struggle between the contestants." The personalized aspect of the violence can be inferred from various reports, in particular, that of the Chicago Commission on Race Relations, which stated that "without the spectators, mob violence would probably have stopped short of murder in many cases." [3]

Directed at specific and visible targets, guns often blazed where one side had the overwhelming advantage. Deaths by beating, nevertheless, greatly outnumbered those from gunshots. Furthermore, the commission found only one serious incident and a number of scattered occurrences where blacks sought to retaliate against white marauders passing by in automobiles. In fact, instead of the term "sniper" fire, many reports of the period around World War I spoke of occasional "volley firing." [4]

Although the Chicago racial rioting may have started

[3] *Ibid.*, 397.
[4] *Ibid.*

in a rumor, the fact remains that at least 36 people died and the number injured totaled 536. Rumor often became the first step in crowd formation and often opened the way for the sharp transformation of a crowd into a mob. The circulation of rumors partly resulted from natural repetition, often with increasing embellishment, by one person to another of what he heard or read. The desire to tell a "big story" and to create a sensation, no doubt, became an important factor in the rioting. With so much bitterness among the antagonists there also appeared considerable conscious effort to provoke "vengeful animosity" by telling the worst that the teller had heard or could imagine about the actions of the opposite race. The latter type of rumor fed the riot from beginning to end and continues to be a constant menace to friendly relations between the races.[5]

The Chicago riot showed, too, that it was unsafe to leave the delicate problem of racial relations, aggravated as they had been by the necessity for assimilating large numbers of immigrants, to those groups of the community mainly interested in exploiting the newcomers for economic and political gain. According to Herbert J. Seligmann, what the racial question needed more than anything else was "rational discussion, a stripping away of the emotional phrases, the sentimen-

---

[5] Thompson and Hughes (eds.), 394–98; Walter F. White, *How Far the Promised Land?* (New York: The Viking Press, 1956), 126, stated that the riot "was sparked by a white property-owners' organization."

tality and the deliberate misrepresentation which obscure the real issues." [6]

As early as April 25, 1919, antagonism prevailed in the vicinity of Fortieth Street and Vincennes Avenue and nearly developed into a riot. Frank Ragan or Patrick McHale, of the Fourth Precinct police station, shot William Epps, black, age twenty-three, of 5700 Wabash Avenue. Near death, Epps was rushed to Provident Hospital by ambulance. After the incident *Defender* reporters made several telephone calls to the precinct station to find out how the affair occurred. Sergeant Jacobs stated that he had not received a report describing the incident. At 10:30 P.M. reporters called him again, nearly three hours after the shooting, and he still professed ignorance of the matter. The reporters then called Acting Captain I. S. Lee, commander of the station, and asked for a report on the shooting of Epps. He stated that he had no knowledge of how the shooting occurred, claiming that the officers had made no report up to that hour, and before the conversation could be concluded, Captain Lee hung up the phone. Later, *Defender* reporters found out that in the vicinity in which the affair occurred a rowdy element of whites constantly beat and slugged black people who passed back and forth in the community, and that this element had the "silent acquiescence of the police in that district." [7]

[6] Seligmann, "Negro Uprising?" 155.
[7] Chicago *Defender*, April 26, 1919.

White hostility toward blacks had been mounting since the 1890's. Although segregation never became formalized, increasing interracial contacts had created a pattern of pervasive discrimination of which the Epps case was only one example. Historically, rising racial tension had been accompanied by periodic outbursts of violence: frequent melees grew out of housing disputes, and the Springfield racial riot of 1908 had provoked violence between blacks and whites in Chicago. The black community, nevertheless, appeared too small to become a major threat before World War I, and only the few whites who had frequent and direct confrontations with black people expressed violent hostilities.[8]

With the ending of the war, the climax to the great southern exodus by blacks, and the return of white veterans looking for jobs and housing, the racial situation in Chicago became extremely intense, with only a spark needed to ignite the huge bonfire of black-white antagonism. Thus on a blisteringly hot Sunday afternoon, July 27, 1919, Eugene Williams, black, drowned at the Twenty-ninth Street beach, touching off the calamity that had so long been feared.[9] The refusal of Policeman Daniel Callahan, white, of the Cottage

[8] Allan H. Spear, *Black Chicago: The Making of a Negro Ghetto, 1890–1920* (Chicago: University of Chicago Press, 1967), 201.

[9] *Ibid.*, 214; on page 184, Spear states that during the riot, the white firm that regularly printed the Chicago *Defender* refused to print the paper for fear of white retaliation. Only by rushing the galleys and newsprint to Gary, Indiana, did its editor, Robert S. Abbott, turn out a riot edition.

Grove station to arrest George Stauber, white, 2904 Cottage Grove Avenue, after he allegedly threw a rock and knocked Williams, age eighteen, 3921 Prairie Avenue, from a raft as it floated down Lake Michigan at Twenty-ninth Street, fanned into action one of the worst racial riots in the history of Illinois. Many witnesses stated that Officer Callahan not only refused to make an arrest but also kept swimmers from reaching Williams. The news of Callahan's malicious negligence reached black bathers at the Twenty-sixth Street beach, and fifty men marched to Twenty-ninth Street to avenge the death of young Williams. The patrolman's action so enraged the bathers that they pounced upon Callahan and "commenced to pommel him." They chased him to a drugstore, where he summoned help. Whites and blacks on the beach clashed, and a "battle royal" raged. Policeman John F. O'Brien, 7151 Michigan Avenue, received a bullet wound in his left arm. During the general melee, Detective Sergeants Middleton and Scott appeared on the scene and placed Stauber under arrest. Whites attempted to take Stauber from the detectives, but the officers held them off at gun point.[10]

After dark, the white gangs west of Wentworth Avenue retaliated against black gangs on the beach by beating, stabbing, or shooting thirty-eight black people who had accidentally wandered into white districts

[10] Chicago *Defender*, August 2, 1919; Graham Taylor, "Chicago in the Nation's Race Strife," *Survey*, XLII (August 9, 1919), 695.

while blacks attacked trolleys and automobiles. Although two people died the first day and over fifty sustained injuries, the Chicago *Tribune* did not even give
the riot a banner headline.[11] The news of Williams's
death spread like wildfire, and around eight o'clock
Sunday night the entire South Side erupted. Blacks
pulled trolleys from their lines in the vicinity of Thirty-
fifth and State Streets, took all white passengers from
the cars, and then severely beat them. They also stopped
automobiles, took the occupants out, and beat them
with sticks. Martin Webb, white, died as a result of
head wounds received in this rampage. To quell the
rioting Sunday night, five hundred patrolmen invaded
the black district and remained there until Monday
morning. At six o'clock Monday morning, whites am-
bushed two black men on their way to work at the
stockyards. Pistols flashed and men made threats of in-
vading the stockyards district where the whites attacked
every black man who came to work. Stores closed and
movie houses boarded up their doors. All women and
children stayed off the streets.[12]

By Monday evening, July 28, Chicago knew that the
catastrophe had really come. Rioting had resumed in the
late afternoon as white gangs assaulted black workers
leaving the stockyards. Mobs pulled streetcars from
their wires and dragged out black passengers, kicking
and beating them. Mobs of black men retaliated and at-

[11] Spear, 214; Waskow, 41.
[12] Chicago *Defender*, August 2, 1919; Tuttle, 209.

tacked whites who worked in the "Black Belt." As
the night expired the white rioters became bolder. They
raided black neighborhoods and fired shots into the
homes and automobiles of black people. During this one
night of terror, the worst period of rioting, twenty
people were killed and hundreds were injured.[13]

Groups of black men gathered on the streets and
discussed the situation. Seeking revenge, the word
passed around was to "clean the district of whites." As
the fever of racial animosity kept gaining ground black
workers from the stockyards returned with stories of
horrible attacks made by white men upon black women.
These rumors so enraged the crowd that they defied
the policemen and beat all white men that they encountered. A crowd swarmed to Thirty-fifth Street
and Wabash Avenue and stopped all streetcars. They
broke windows in the cars with brickbats and sticks.
Reports stated that during this attack whites sympathiz-
ing with occupants in the streetcars endeavored to
disperse the crowd by hurling tin cans and other articles
down on the attackers from the Angeles Building, an
apartment house on the corner of Thirty-fifth Street
and Wabash. The rioters turned to the building and
smashed a number of windows in flats said to be occupied by white families. Police persuasion kept the
mob from entering the building. At this point the police

[13] Spear, 214–15; Leslie H. Fishel, Jr., and Benjamin Quarles, *The
Negro American: A Documentary History* (Glenview, Ill.: Scott,
Foresman, 1967), 413.

realized the smallness of their group, and a general-riot call went out, the first in the history of the city since the famous Haymarket riot.

Several newspapers and many civic leaders demanded that Mayor Bill Thompson ask Governor Frank Lowden for a detachment of state militia. The governor, responding promptly to the outbreak of hostilities, ordered the mobilization of several companies of militia and stationed them at nearby amories, but he could send them into the streets only at the mayor's request. Throughout Monday night and all of Tuesday, both the mayor and the chief of police insisted that the local forces held "full command," and that no outside assistance would be necessary. Black leaders hesitated to request the militia because they recalled that state forces had supported the white mobs in East St. Louis in 1917. Furthermore, shortly after Monday night's hostilities had ended news of the death of Policeman John H. Simpson, age thirty-one, 3910 Calumet Avenue, of the Forty-eighth Street police station, became public knowledge; this news reinforced the blacks' suspicions of reprisal from policemen and militiamen. Shot at Thirty-first and Wabash Avenue by a black rioter, he died shortly after at Mercy Hospital.[14]

Rioting continued on Tuesday, July 29, and spread beyond the South Side. At Forty-seventh and State Streets the rioters started the battle again; their activities

[14] Chicago *Defender*, August 2, 1919; Spear, 215.

spread from Forty-seventh to Fifty-third Streets. Police shot down a black youth with a gun, an incident which attracted several hundred people, mostly white. Automobiles whisked through the crowded streets with their occupants firing right and left. Several white men fell wounded. The cars made their way to Fifty-first Street, where their occupants turned the district into a "no man's land." A white driver of a packing company truck, passing through the riot zone, received several bullet wounds that resulted in his death. The police ordered Fifty-first Street closed to all traffic, and the scene of racial warfare drifted back to Forty-seventh Street, where a general rocking of automobiles, even police cars, started.[15]

Black men enroute on foot to and from their jobs through the hostile territory of the "Loop" faced death. White soldiers and sailors in uniform, aided by civilians, raided the "Loop" business section, killing two blacks and beating and robbing several others. Blacks living in predominantly white neighborhoods in Englewood, far to the south, had to flee their homes as whites stole their household goods and burned or wrecked their homes. On the West Side, an Italian mob, excited by a false rumor that an Italian girl had been shot by a black, killed a black man named Joseph Lovings. Raids into the black residential areas continued. Automobiles sped through the streets, the riders shooting at random.

[15] Chicago *Defender*, August 2, 1919; Taylor, 696.

Blacks retaliated by sniping from ambush. Surface and elevated car service stopped because a strike for wage increases kept thousands of employees from work.[16]

The situation reached such a point that civic leaders issued circulars pleading for order. The police had matters under control until 6:00 P.M. Wednesday, at which time things took a turn for the worst. Rumors spread through the South Side district stating that whites on Wentworth Avenue had assembled to invade State Street. At the corner of Thirty-fifth and State Streets several black men reportedly exhibited hand grenades in preparation for the attack, although over 500 policemen, mounted and on foot, had been stationed at Thirty-first and Thirty-fifth Streets. Police received orders to "shoot to kill" any person who tried to provoke a disturbance. When night came police ordered all businesses catering to the public closed.

Everything seemed quiet until 9:15 P.M. Suddenly a horde of automobiles wheeled around the corner at Twenty-sixth and State Streets, loaded with white men carrying army rifles and an unlimited amount of ammunition. Speeding down the street at a rate of approximately fifty miles an hour the riders fired wildly in all directions. The cars slowed down at Thirty-seventh Street on State Street, and the occupants fired into a crowd of black men. Motorcycle policemen picked up

16 Spear, 214; Fishel and Quarles, 413; Taylor, 696; Chicago Commission on Race Relations, *The Negro in Chicago* (Chicago: University of Chicago Press, 1922), 585.

their trails at Thirty-fifth Street and closed in on them between Thirty-seventh and Thirty-eighth Streets. One of the cars stopped at Thirty-ninth Street. Three of its occupants lay dead on the back seat, and two others emerged seriously wounded. Five minutes later another automobile swung out and its riders started firing right and left. The policemen at Thirty-fifth Street, warned of this attack, placed their patrol wagons across the street and blocked the path of the automobile. A fusillade of shots greeted the car's occupants, and four men in it died. Another "death car" followed this one coming from Root Street and headed for Thirty-ninth Street. Ambulances took several of the wounded to Provident Hospital for treatment. When a group of black men heard of this action, they headed for the hospital and threatened to batter the doors down to get to the whites. Here someone shot and slightly wounded Detective Sergeant Middleton.[17]

Finally, at 10:30 P.M. on Wednesday, with the worst already over, Mayor Thompson asked Governor Lowden to send in the militia. Unlike the guardsmen used at East St. Louis, the troops that entered Chicago had been especially trained for riot duty and performed well. They prevented the formation of mobs and marauding parties. Rain and cooler temperatures on Thursday and Friday, together with the work of the militia, quelled the rioting. Early Saturday morning, in-

[17] Chicago *Defender*, August 2, 1919.

cendiary fires destroyed forty-nine homes in the immi-
grant community west of the stockyards and left 948
Lithuanians homeless, with a loss in property of more
than $250,000. Responsibility for the fires was never
ascertained. Despite angry accusations that blacks
seemed guilty, rioting did not resume.[18]

The governor never did impose martial law during
the Chicago riot, but in other respects the South Side
resembled a beseiged city. Most blacks could not get
to work because of the streetcar strike, and to venture
outside the "Black Belt" on foot continued to be unsafe
after dark. Black leaders urged everyone to stay off the
streets. Moreover, white deliverymen and shopkeepers,
fearing retaliation, refused to enter the black section,
and in many areas the food supply nearly stopped. To
meet these emergencies the Red Cross and the Urban
League distributed food to needy families, and the
packing companies set up pay stations on the South Side
so that black employees, unable to get to the stockyards,
would not be without funds.[19]

The Chicago riot turned out to be a "two-sided conflict," with members of both races committing acts of
wanton cruelty. Nevertheless, all objective observers
agreed not only that whites must assume responsibility
for the atrocious acts that led to the rioting but also
for being the aggressors during the riot itself. Blacks

[18] Spear, 214–15; Fishel and Quarles, 413.
[19] Spear, 215–16; "Race Riots in Washington and Chicago," *Current History*, X (September, 1919), 454.

assuredly killed and maimed innocent whites who came into the black section, but unlike the white gangs that invaded black neighborhoods, blacks rarely stormed white districts to commit violent deeds.

The charges that blacks burned the houses near the stockyards proved unfounded, and several witnesses reported seeing "white men with blackened faces" in the area at the time of the fires. Furthermore, black violence generally took the form of individual attack because there existed no organized black gangs bent on furthering racial conflict.[20] Responsibility for many attacks thus was definitely placed by many witnesses upon the white "athletic clubs," including "Ragan's Colts," the "Hamburgers," "Aylwards," "Our Flag," the "Standard," the "Sparklers" and several others. The mobs consisted for the most part of boys between the ages of fifteen and twenty-two. Older persons participated, but the youth of the rioters became conspicuous in every clash. Little children witnessed the brutalities and frequently pointed out assailants to police officers.

The final casualty figures also indicated that blacks had been more the victims than the attackers: 23 blacks and 15 whites dead; 342 blacks and 178 whites injured. Forty-one per cent of the reported clashes occurred in the white neighborhood near the stockyards, between the south branch of the city limits; and 34 per cent in the "Black Belt," between Twenty-second and

[20] Seligmann, "Negro Uprisings?" 155; Spear, 216; Grimshaw, 68.

Thirty-ninth Streets, Wentworth Avenue and Lake Michigan, while the rest were scattered around the city. The grand jury that investigated the riot concluded that "the colored people suffered more at the hands of white hoodlums than the white people suffered at the hands of black hoodlums." Yet, many whites reacted to the riot, not by reproaching the antiblack elements, but by urging stricter racial segregation.[21]

White policemen in certain districts where the rioters staged their battles were criticized for arresting only blacks participating in violent activities. Judge William Nelson Gemmill of the Hyde Park Court discharged twenty black prisoners called before him on the theory that they could not have been fighting among themselves and ordered the police department to "bring him some white prisoners." After a coroner's inquest declared that the stone thrown by George Stauber did not cause Eugene Williams's drowning, the former was released from custody.

Illinois Attorney General Maclay Hoyne displayed extreme prejudice and suffered a severe reprimand from the grand jury after evidence proved that he had no intention of prosecuting white rioters, and the grand jury demanded that he present evidence involving white rioters.[22] Hoyne further demonstrated his bias in quotations attributed to him in the *Literary Digest*. At the

[21] Fishel and Quarles, 414; "Race Riots in Washington and Chicago," 454; Spear, 217.
[22] Chicago *Defender*, August 9, 1919.

time of the rioting he found that blacks were the aggressors in the "race war" because organization leaders
in city hall, black and white, "had catered to the
vicious elements of the black race for the past six years."
Teaching the blacks to look jokingly upon the law and
that they should ignore policemen if they had political
backing allowed black criminality to reign. The prose-
cutor charged that black politicians had even threatened the discharge of white police officers who arrested
favored and protected black law breakers. He insisted
that the "ignorant blacks" imported from the South
listened to false teachings upon their arrival in Chicago
and threw off all restraint. He also blamed the tense
racial feelings upon the lack of sufficient segregated
housing for the growing black population, which led to
an invasion of many residential areas previously restricted to whites. Hoyne's remedy for the situation
called for an immediate increase in the police force,
the declaration of martial law, and a search of buildings
in the "Black Belt" to remove "firearms, deadly weapons, and ammunition now stored there in large quan-
tities." Finally, he proposed a "scheme of segregation, to
which the majority of the black people will themselves
consent." [23]

But aside from general lawlessness and disastrous violence that preceded the Chicago riot and those factors
pointed out by Maclay Hoyne, other factors arose. In

[23] "Why the Negro Appeals to Violence," *Literary Digest*, LXII
(August 9, 1919), 11; see app. E.

Chicago considerable unrest had been occasioned in industry by increasing competition between white and black laborers following the sudden increase in the black population. Hoyne was correct in saying that this increase developed a housing crisis whereby the blacks overflowed the hitherto all-white residential areas and moved into all white neighborhoods, resulting in greatly increased racial tension.

In the two years just preceding the riot, twenty-seven black dwellings were wrecked by bombs thrown by unidentified persons.[24] Willis N. Huggins, editor of the black weekly, Chicago *Searchlight*, ascribed the origin of the racial feud to the large employers of labor who had "imported thousands of blacks into the city" and to the city's failure to provide housing accommodations. He also referred to political exploitations by local leaders, to unscrupulous landlords' profiteering, and to sensational articles in the public press of the country.

E. Frank Gardiner, in a long article in the *New York Times*, lay stress upon the linking of corrupt politics with gambling houses and other places of ill fame where lower-class blacks and whites "drank and danced together all night undisturbed by the mayor or by the city police."[25] An anonymous writer added another explanation when he stated that petty quarreling, occasional shooting affrays, and street fights between blacks and whites in Chicago had been sufficiently nu-

---

[24] Chicago Commission on Race Relations, 596.
[25] "Race Riots in Washington and Chicago," 454.

merous to indicate unusually strained racial relations caused, in large part, by "the increased self-assertiveness of the black people." [26]

According to Herbert J. Seligmann, the relations of the races had become a national problem. Black people did not constitute that problem, but "the attitude of the white man towards them" did. The white South still envisaged that problem in terms of racial inferiority, social inequality, black criminality, and rape. But in Chicago the words most often used in accounting for the bitter feelings which existed happened not to be black criminality or brutal assaults upon white women, but "decline of real estate values, invasion of white residential districts by blacks, and friction between union men and ununionized blacks." Furthermore, when blacks moved into white residential districts, there began talk of "segregation" and white property owners' associations indulged in incendiary language at meetings that were often secret.[27]

As soon as the riot ended, the indefatigable Walter F. White investigated the situation in Chicago for four weeks and concluded that its causes were similar to what existed in every large city with a large black population. He identified eight formal causes for the atrocities and listed them according to their importance. They were, racial prejudice, economic competition, political corruption and exploitation of black voters,

[26] "Darkest Cloud," *Survey*, XLII (August 2, 1919), 676.
[27] Seligmann, "Negro Uprisings?" 154.

police inefficiency, newspaper "lies" about black crimes, unpublished crimes against black people, housing, and the reaction of white and black veterans.

Equally important as a cause for the racial unrest, although seldom considered, is the fact that many southern whites also went to the North, many of them to Chicago, drawn by the same economic advantages that attracted the black workman. The exact figure remains unknown, but estimates state that more than 20,000 southern whites went to Chicago during the war years. These whites spread "the virus of racial hatred," and evidences of it could be seen all over Chicago. This same cause underlay each of White's other eight causes.[28]

Chief of Police John J. Garrity, in explaining the inability of the police to curb the rioters, said the force could not adequately police one-third of the city. Aside from this fact, blacks distrusted white police officers, and implications by the chief and statements by State's Attorney Hoyne proved that many of the police were "grossly unfair in making arrests." The commission established instances of actual police participation in the rioting as well as neglect of duty. Of 229 persons arrested and accused of various criminal activities during the riot, 154 were black and 75 were white. Of those indicted, 81 were black and 47 were white. Although these figures would indicate greater riot activity on the

[28] Walter F. White, "Chicago and Its Eight Reasons," *Crisis*, (1919), 293–94.

part of black people, further reports of clashes showed that of 520 persons injured, 342 turned out to be black and only 178 white. That twice as many blacks appeared as defendants and twice as many blacks as whites sustained injuries leads one to conclude that whites were not apprehended as readily as blacks. Furthermore, many of the depredations that occurred outside the "Black Belt" were encouraged by the absence of policemen. Out of a force of 3,000 policemen, 2,800 massed in the "Black Belt" during the height of the rioting. In the "Loop" district, where two black men encountered death and several others received numerous wounds, there were only three patrolmen and one sergeant. Nor had the police adequately staffed the stockyards district.[29]

Other factors leading to the rioting were discussed in an article by Charles W. Holman. He stated that troubled relations became noticeable in 1917 when black people began to compose an important part of the street and elevated railway traffic. The blacks strung themselves through the trains or cars in such a way that the "whites thought they did it on purpose to force the whites to sit down besides them." This action caused much resentment, and it became apparent that trouble loomed. Rumors also stated that many apartments were rented to blacks by whites for "spite reasons," and that certain classes of whites had not hesitated to grant

[29] Chicago Commission on Race Relations, 599.

blacks absolute social equality. In the black section white girls walked with black men and white men paraded the streets with black women. They even intermarried! [30]

Added to Holman's comments were those of Graham Taylor, who stated that "insufficient and unsuitable housing provisions" for the industrial classes must be considered the economic factor of the racial problem which gave occasion for the outbreaks of resentment and violence because it bore heaviest upon the blacks and most irritated the whites. The district in which Chicago blacks could find available dwellings most easily happened to be located, unfortunately, at the older center of a growing section of town which afforded no space for the spread of the increasingly congested black population. With the doubling of that population, the congestion became intolerable, forcing the families to seek residence elsewhere. Despite an overcharge of from 15 per cent to 25 per cent on rentals and sales of real estate, adjacent properties occupied by whites depreciated in value. Resentment against those thought guilty of this intrusion and loss not only prevented neighborliness, but incited persecution. Bombs were the deterrents used before the riot; the torch, when the mob got control. Capitalists interested in the solution of this housing problem insisted that "the rentals which black laborers can pay will not return 5 per cent

[30] Holman, "Race Riots in Chicago," *Outlook*, CXXII (August 13, 1919), 567.

on the investment, which therefore cannot be considered as a business proposition in real estate." Self-respecting blacks resented its consideration upon any other basis and insisted that a single demonstration that such an investment might have met with a warrantable return would be followed by others bringing about the speedy solution of the housing problem. In any event, concluded Taylor, the housing crisis forced the conviction that some way had to be found other than "that worse laissez faire policy, which proved to be no way at all." [31]

Many factors, therefore, proved potent matches igniting the flames of racial war in Chicago. Despite the community's failure to deal firmly with those who disturbed its peace and contributed to the reign of terror and lawlessness that shamed Chicago before mankind, evidence persists that the riot aroused many citizens of both races to a "quickened sense of suffering and disgrace." This shame had come once and possibly would return. Many citizens developed "a determination to prevent a recurrence of so disastrous an outbreak of racial hatred" and world-wide disgrace.

This spirit manifested itself on at least three occasions in 1920 when, confronted suddenly with events out of which serious riots might easily have grown, people of both races acted with such courage and promptness that the troubles ended early or never got started.[32] Chi-

[31] Taylor, 696.
[32] Fishel and Quarles, 415.

cagoans came to feel that harmony rather than strife and racial war could cause more community good than harm, and many worked to see that the days of racial peace might not have to suffer the setting of the sun.

# CHAPTER VI

# Conclusion

This book proves that blacks were the victims of these riots and that an underlying cause was racial tension between blacks and whites. It is, however, equally important to point out differing reasons for each conflict. The Knoxville, Tennessee, riot found its motivation in sexual criminality, while the Elaine, Arkansas, situation turned on economic betterment and repression. The Tulsa, Oklahoma, problem hinged on sexual, social, and economic inequities; and the Chicago, Illinois, riot sprang from white and black economic competition and social injustice. Even though these different causes are apparent, there remain glaring similarities which underlay the racial riots in Knoxville, Elaine, Tulsa, and Chicago—all arising from the troubled times of our racially torn American past.

The end of World War I in November, 1918, did not bring social peace to America. It opened a period in which social groups fought against each other in struggles that often broke into bloody conflict. The migration of blacks to the North during the war years ended in a series of racial riots in northern cities. Blacks on the move in the South caused whites there to fear change and forced them to react with lynchings and racial wars to keep the blacks down. Significant clashes occurred between labor and capital and between conservative and radical points of view. In addition, the rise of the

Ku Klux Klan divided Americans religiously and socially and pitted rural, small-town America against urban America. Released from wartime controls, American labor union demanded higher wages to match the ever increasing cost of living. As American industry fought to preserve the prevailing wage level and the nonunion shop, regional labor dislocations, general strikes, and violence formed a national pattern.[1]

A myriad of factors, therefore, suggest causes for rioting and racial violence. Continued wartime migration of many southern blacks to the North, inadequate housing for blacks, wartime intolerance, high rents, inefficiency of the police, white-black economic competition, a feeling of independence on the part of certain blacks, and, inevitably, bolshevism. Riots in factory towns in Pennsylvania and New Jersey in 1917, and in Knoxville, Elaine, Chicago, Omaha, and Washington D.C., in 1919, convinced the white South that racial violence was national and not sectional. According to their expectations, when blacks moved northward racial riots would follow. Then too, by 1919 blacks, along with other minority groups, were beginning to create a new America, one which would force most whites to change their thought and action processes. Whites, not wanting to change, reacted violently.[2]

[1] George E. Mowry, "The Twenties: The Limits of Freedom," in Richard W. Leopold, Arthur S. Link, and Stanley Coben (eds.), *Problems in American History*, Vol. II (Englewood Cliffs: Prentice-Hall, 1966), 240–41.
[2] Robert K. Murray, *Red Scare: A Study in National Hysteria,*

Racial riots are the dramatic hallmark of the injustices of racial relations in America. During World War I and its aftermath, the modern form of the racial riot developed in northern and border cities where blacks attempted to alter their position of subordination. Furthermore, the riots of this period may be called "communal" riots or "contested area" riots. They involved ecological warfare, because they became a direct struggle between the residents of white and black areas, and the precipitating incidents came after a period of increased tension and occasional minor but persistent outbreaks of violence.[3]

Racial prejudice, compounded through the years, seemed to reach a peak between 1919 and 1921. Whites despised blacks because of their color and supposed threat to the existence and continuation of the white race. Black men were made to appear as brutal savages out to rape white women or demean them in the eyes of the white man.

The white man put his woman on a pedestal and protected her with an insane passion. He castrated, lynched, and legally murdered black men who chanced to glance her way. Black women became animals instead

*1919–1920* (Minneapolis: University of Minnesota Press, 1955), 178; Preston W. Slosson, *The Great Crusade and After, 1914–28* (New York: The Macmillan Company, 1930), 258; Williard B. Gatewood, Jr., *Controversy in the Twenties: Fundamentalism, Modernism, and Evolution* (Nashville: Vanderbilt University Press, 1969), 18.

[3] National Commission on the Causes and Prevention of Violence, June 1969, 393–96.

of women, and the white man abused them in every way while his female counterpart sat sexually frustrated upon her ivory throne. Miscegenation was forbidden, but 70 per cent[4] of the black race contains white blood. Prejudice aided southern white men in their equation of the southern white woman with the noble and sacred South, and, as W. J. Cash suggests, white men in the South developed a rape complex. If a black man allegedly raped or insulted a white woman, he also presumably raped or insulted the virgin South. To avenge these crimes whites, South and North, lynched blacks.

When lynching came under national attack a new form of revenge became prominent. In order to kick blacks back into their place, riots occurred in both the North and the South. Other factors contributed to the need for riots to put down the black menace, but the fact remains that racial prejudice, with all its stimuli, psychologically motivated whites either to eliminate or to subjugate further the upward-bound black population. As this population strove to attain the goals of the great democratic experience, whites saw that their American dream would collapse, ending the white domination that has existed in America for more than four hundred years.

The frustration of seeing his kingdom begin to come tumbling down piece by piece through economic, political, judicial, and social equality, caused the white man

4 Myrdal, 133.

to try to mend the cracks by becoming the aggressor in the racial riots of the postwar years. Blacks were machine gunned, burned out of their homes, bombed, lynched, beaten, stabbed, and mutilated in the most gruesome fashions. This violence was deemed necessary to entrench in the black mind the white-imposed fact that blacks must remain docile, childlike, submissive, subservient, and in their proper place—that is, under the heel of their white benefactors.

This frustration, therefore, made fear the prime element in black control. Fear of what blacks might accomplish led whites to the conclusion that fear of white power by blacks would do more to subjugate the black race than any other method and would also save face in the international community. The acts of rioting and instilling fear also satisfied a sadistic lust and paternalistic desire to aid but dominate the physical and mental being of black Americans. Whites reasoned that blacks could not get along in this white man's country without the white man's benevolent aid, and that the best way to make the blacks see this fact was to scare them into a psychological acceptance of anything the great white father might do.

Excerpt from a speech by Senator John Sharp Williams, made on the floor of the United States Senate, September 29, 1919 and cited in the article "Mob Rule As a National Menace," *Literary Digest*, LXIII (October 18, 1919), 11.

I go as far in the pathways of peace as any man who was ever born. I am willing to arbitrate nearly everything in this world, except one thing, and that is the attempt to outrage a white woman by any man, either white, black, or red. I surrender him at once as being beyond the pale of the law, to the first crowd that can get to him. I believe in law. I believe in law and order. I believe that there is no justification for taking the law into one's own hands. But I believe that there are now and then provocation and excuse enough for it . . . .

Not only is blood thicker than water, but race is greater than law, now and then; and if race be not greater than law, about which there might be a dispute, the protection of a woman transcends all law of every description, human or divine.

"Returning Soldiers" by William E. B. DuBois, cited in Leslie H. Fishel, Jr. and Benjamin Quarles, *The Negro American: A Documentary History*. Glenview, Ill.: Scott, Foresman, 1967, 410–12.

We are returning from the war! The Crisis of tens of thousands of black men were drafted into a great struggle. For bleeding France and what she means and has meant and will mean to us and humanity and against the threat of German race arrogance, we fought gladly and to the last drop of blood; for America and her highest ideal, we fought in far-off hope; for the dominant southern oligarchy entrenched in Washington, we fought in bitter resignation. For the America that represents and gloats in lynching, disfranchisement, caste, brutality and devilish insult—for this, in the hateful upturning and mixing of things, we were forced by vindictive fate to fight also.

But today we return! We return from the slavery of uniform which the world's madness demanded us to don to the freedom of civil garb. We stand again to look America squarely in the face and call a spade a spade. We sing: This country of ours, despite all its better souls have done and dreamed, is yet a shameful land.

It *lynches*.

And lynching is barbarism of a degree of contemptible nastiness unparalleled in human history. Yet for fifty years we have lynched two blacks a week, and we have kept this up right through the war.

It *disfranchises* its own citizens.

Disfranchisement is the deliberate theft and robbery of the only protection of poor against rich and black against white. The land that disfranchises its citizens and calls itself a democracy lies and knows it lies.

It encourages *ignorance*.

It has never really tried to educate the black people. A dominant minority does not want blacks educated. It wants servants, dogs, whores and monkeys. And when this land allows a reactionary group by its stolen political power to force as many black folk into categories as it possibly can, it cries in contemptible hypocrisy: "they threaten us with degeneracy; they cannot be educated."

It *steals* from us.

It organizes industry to cheat us. It cheats us out of our land; it cheats us out of our labor. It confiscates our savings. It reduces our wages. It raises our rent. It steals our profit. It taxes us without representation. It keeps us consistently and universally poor, and then feeds us on charity and derides our poverty.

It *insults* us.

It has organized nation-wide and latterly a world-wide propaganda of deliberate and continuous insult and defamation
of black blood wherever found. It decrees that it shall not be
possible in travel nor residence, work nor play, education nor
instruction for a black man to exist without tacit or open
acknowledgement of his inferiority to the dirtiest white dog.
And it looks upon any attempt to question or even discuss this
dogma as arrogance, unwarranted assumption and treason.

This is the country to which we Soldiers of Democracy return. This is the fatherland for which we fought! But it is
*our* fatherland. It was right for us to fight. The faults of *our*
country are *our* faults. Under similar circumstances, we would
fight again. But by the God of Heaven, we are cowards and
jackasses if now that war is over, we do not marshal every
ounce of our brain and brawn to fight a sterner, longer, more
unbending battle against the forces of hell in our own land.

We *return.*

We *return from fighting.*

We *return fighting.*

Make way for Democracy! We saved it in France, and by
the Great Jehovah, we will save it in the United States of
America, or know the reason why.

APPENDIX B

Proclamation of Major John E. McMillan of Knoxville,
Tennessee, taken from Knoxville *Journal and Tribune,*
September 1, 1919, 1.

To the people of Knoxville:

After the terrible experiences that have confronted us during
the past few hours—when reason seemed to be dethroned and
law forgotten and overridden—I appeal to your reason and conscience for counsel and aid that there may be quiet and modera-
tion upon the part of all classes of citizens. A horrible crime

upon an innocent woman is well calculated to arouse the primeval passion of men and to lead to hasty action outside the law; but the majesty of the law must be sustained and the fair name of Knoxville and her wonderful history for law and order and for law enforcement must not be allowed to be tarnished and our good citizens caused to be shamed by any lawless element in our midst.

Passions and hates are the spirit of the mob and law defiance the black current underlying mob violence, but the laws of our state must be upheld against all odds and therefore, it behooves all our people, irrespective of race or color, to let reason and conscience resume their sway and control and to endeavor by every means to subdue and remove the passions of the hour and to stand as a bulwark for law and order against the lawless elements of both races responsible for the unhappy conditions and troubles thrust upon us.

Last night the Adjutant General of the state in command of the national guards encamped near our city at the request of county officials, and I am informed, brought officers and sol-· diers into our city and states that he will patrol our streets until order is restored. For all aid he may give the city our citizens will be thankful.

Last night the whole police force of the city were [sic] called out and on duty doing their [sic] utmost to prevent violations of any man's property or liberties. This, Sunday afternoon, the board of commissioners have [sic] held a special meeting and unanimously voted to have sworn in 150 special policemen and large numbers are now being sworn in and the whole number will, before morning, be on duty to guard and defend your persons and property and to prevent repetition of lawlessness.

A few hours of quiet and sane counsel will restore order and rebuke lawlessness, and I beg that all classes of citizens co-operate with the officers of the law and in so far as possible remain at their homes or about their usual avocations and aid in preventing lawlessness and unlawful gatherings which may result in new disorders.

A heinous crime has been committed but that is no justification for lawlessness though [it is] often made the pretext for mob violence and plunder of property and injury and insult to innocent and inoffensive citizens.

I appeal to you for aid that the orderly processes of the law be carried out and you may be sure that a Knox county jury will mete out swift and just punishment to the guilty.

Again I beg that you co-operate with the officials of the city to suppress all attempts to arouse feeling between any classes of our citizens regardless of race or color.

I call upon the cool, level-headed citizens of all races and classes to co-operate with me in the restoration of order, peace and safety and to aid officials, both city and state, to bring lawful and swift punishment to all who defy the laws of our state and bring reproach upon the name of our fair city.

This August 31, 1919.

Statement of W. L. Porter, editor of the *East Tennessee News*, a black newspaper, and local black leader. This statement was taken from the Knoxville *Journal and Tribune*, September 2, 1919, 2.

As the news of the crime committed in our city spread and reached the ears of the negroes of the community, it produced a great shock and was as much deplored by the members of the race as by the nearest relative of the unfortunate victim, especially since suspicion points toward a negro. The sentiment of the entire race is voiced when I state that crime should be punished to the fullest extent of the law, regardless as to whether the perpetrator of the deed is white or black and the statements generally heard coming from thoughtful members of the race favored inflicting the full penalty of the law as soon as the guilt of the accused is definitely established. Not only is there no inclination on the part of the thoughtful law abiding negroes to condone crime, but there are many of those in our city, among the leaders of the race who are continually waging a fight against the presence in the community of the crime-breeding dives where vulgar actions exist and plans for crimes are born. The thought paramount in the minds of the law abiding negroes of our city, who are interested in the welfare of the entire populace, is to lend every assistance to the officials in suppressing crime and when any act is committed by a member of the race, there are just as many negroes who will give aid to the proper officials in apprehending the perpetrator of the deed, as of any other race. The friendly relationship between the races that has existed in our section can be attributed to the absence of just such deeds as has been committed and the negro citizenship is certainly desirous of retaining the same cordial feeling between the races as has always existed and that has gone so far in making our city one fit to live in. It is sincerely hoped, as terrible and deplorable as the crime may be, that the saner judgment will prevail on the part of all and that the law will be allowed to take its course.

Statement of Police Chief Haynes with reference to the hammerless thirty-eight calibre Smith and Wesson revolver found in the room of Maurice Mays, cited in Knoxville *Journal and Tribune*, August 31, 1919.

I have had some experience with revolvers and can say that a pistol [that] has not been used in some time will invariably have some lint, which comes from the clothing in the barrel. The Mays pistol had been recently fired as every evidence of this was visible at the time it was placed in my hands. The officers who found the pistol in the room say it smelled of fresh powder burns.

Statement of Adjutant General E. B. Sweeney to the crowd at the Knox County jail upon the arrival of his troops, cited in Knoxville *Journal and Tribune*, September 2, 1919, 2.

Men, those men on the hill (referring to the soldiers) have their guns loaded, and are ready to fire. But I have given instructions that no shot shall be fired tonight, and that no death can be blamed on the soldiers. I have as much respect for a white woman as any man in the south. The negro who committed the murder this morning should be hanged. Hell is too good for him. I can promise you that when the man is tried that Governor Roberts will not extend clemency, but he will permit the full punishment of the law.

Editorial comment in the Memphis *Commercial Appeal*, October 3, 1919, p. 6, entitled "Punish the Agitators."

If there be any one of either white or black skin anywhere in the south who is guilty of trying to arouse racial antagonism and strife such person or persons should be immediately ferreted out and punished for their traitorous crime. Any and all agitators to racial violence are infinitely worse than the poor deluded followers who are led to their own destruction. No motive whatever can serve in the least to extenuate the foul crime of such conspirators.

There is no disputing the fact that the races can get along in the south in peace and harmony if the baleful influence of the agitators is removed. Any and all persons who preach any sort of class strife in this country are traitors, not merely to the section where they operate, but to the whole country. They should be deprived of their power of evil, and they will be whenever they show their heads in the light.

APPENDIX C

Speech of Congressman Thaddeus H. Caraway of Arkansas, made on the floor of the House of Representatives, placed in U.S., *Congressional Record*, LVIII (November 19, 1919), 8818 and 8821.

Mr. Speaker and gentlemen of the House, I ask for this time merely to read a press report of a telegram sent to President Wilson and to make a brief statement about an occurrence that took place in my district recently. I have not discussed it before, because there were features about it that I did not care to inject into discussions on this floor.

A negro organization in Phillips County, Ark., had planned to kill the owners of plantations and to take possession of the land. In that county the population is largely black; in some communities there are more than 10 negroes to 1 white person. It is one of the old counties of the State, and to the credit of its splendid citizenship there has never been a lynching within the county. There has never heretofore been friction between the negroes and the white people living in that county. It is a law-abiding community. Growing out of this insurrection there were a number of lives lost, both white and black. Later something like a hundred negroes were arrested. They admitted the organization of a plot and their intention to assassinate the landowners. There was strong pressure from the more hot-headed part of the population to take the law into their own hands as to some of the accused, among them two white lawyers, who seemed to have been mixed up in the conspiracy, and lynch them. But the officials preserved order. No man suffered at the hands of a mob. Everyone connected with the riot who has been arrested had his case submitted to the grand jury. Some of them were indicted and have been tried. Among these were 11 negroes who were admitted to be ringleaders and who had participated in the fight that resulted in the killing of one soldier of the United States, one ex-soldier, several deputy sheriffs, and a number of citizens who were summoned by the sheriff of the county and were commissioned as deputy sheriffs and were trying to make arrests of people who had violated the law. Eleven of these negroes so arrested were sentenced to death.

There is in New York City an association called the National Association for the Advancement of Colored People. I think its correct title should be "An association for the promotion of revolution and inciting to riots."

Let me add but a few words in reference to Phillips County. As I said, it is one of the oldest counties in the State. It was settled long before the Civil War by people of education and means. It has been the birthplace and home of statesmen, authors, soldiers, and men and women prominent in every walk of life. As an illustration, Helena, now a splendid city of 20,000 people, at the beginning of the war between the States, had a population not exceeding 2,500. Three-fifths of these at least were slaves. Yet it furnished to the Confederate Army seven generals. Among these were Gens. Cleburne, Hinemon, Tappan, Govan, and others. Those not mentioned were equally as deserving as those whose names are given. In civil life it has given to the State governors, Senators of the United States, judges of the highest courts, and men and women renowned in every field of intellectual accomplishment.

It should not be traduced by a society whose chief activities have been, as I suggested, to promote revolutions and incite riots....

This society I mentioned appeals to the governor of my State and to the President of the United States to stay the execution of these confessed criminals, and makes the statement that no punishment has been meted out to white persons engaged in the riot. There were no white persons on the scene except commissioned officers, who were deputized to preserve order. No white person had incited to riot except two whites who were alien to that community and have been indicted. No others were mixed up in the riot, if you can call it a riot, except these two white men and the negroes who undertook to overthrow the local government. These negroes were given a fair trial in the court of justice and convicted by a jury. No appeal was taken by them from these verdicts, although they were represented by able lawyers. There was not a line of evidence offered that anyone could believe that tended to show they were not guilty of a conspiracy to murder, and had, in fact, committed murder. And yet this society sends broadcasts throughout the land for an appeal to the President to immediately investigate the situation down there. Now, heretofore, this society has contended that it wanted the law enforced; that it wanted an end to lynching. Here is a county that refused to permit any harm to come to any of these people. No punishment of any kind was or is to be inflicted on them except through the courts, the legally organized tribunals; notwithstanding this, this society now slanders the people of this community and gives utterance to this falsehood. It is apparent that agitation and not justice is desired.

Mercy and not harshness has been manifested by the people of Phillips County, but justice is not the aim of this society whose telegram was the occasion of these remarks. It thrives financially by falsehoods and antagonisms. If people who know nothing of conditions take time to ascertain the truth, societies like this would cease to exist. Its membership is composed of but two classes. One class is desirous of meddling with affairs of which it knows nothing—merely to be in the public eye— the other seeks advantages for itself, whatever harm may follow.

## APPENDIX D

Editorial comment by William B. Smith, of *The Pitchfork*, Dallas, Texas, cited in the Chicago *Defender*, July 9, 1921.

Tulsa, Oklahoma, has been sowing the wind. Just the other day she reaped the Whirlwind. For many years Negro arrogance and impudence has [sic] been increasing through the state of Oklahoma. In Tulsa it was especially noticeable. Finally Negro arrogance became so bold that a few "prominent" coons of that city armed themselves and went to the county jail, demanding the release of another Negro who was being held on a charge of rape. An innocent onlooker, standing on the steps of the court house, fell to his death from the first shots fired by the Negroes. Then, of course, the battle was on. A hundred or more lives were destroyed and a million and a half dollars worth of property was burned.

The story is familiar to all readers of the daily papers. The point I would make is this: If the white people of Tulsa had started a good many years ago to teach its coon population there would be no monkey business tolerated; if the white people of Tulsa had made it plain that white supremacy would suffer no encroachment, instead of giving the Negro population another foot of rope each year, there would have been no such orgy of blood letting and property destruction as above mentioned.

The "race problem" is progressing. Each year the Negro element grows more bold. Their conceit is fed on political patronage. Year by year, office holders become more cowardly in facing the problem. They need Negro votes on election day. And now, since the Negro woman can vote, and since they can be "herded" by the leaders of their race and voted virtually as a body, the Negro vote is [a] definite and valuable element in the political equation. If this evolution in our politics continues, there is going to be hell to pay and no credit granted. Coddling the coon for his vote is only stirring up wrath for the final day of judgment. For this is a white man's country and by God it's going to continue to be!

In some part of the country the white element may "mess along" with the Negro but finally the Negro becomes so intolerable that the white man balks, and—there is a tragedy like the Tulsa affair. How infinitely better it would be if the white man, everywhere, deals with the Negro as the white man deals with him in the South—with kindness, but with absolutely no toleration of any species of impudence! Then there would be no race riots. We don't have any of them in the South. It is true that during the last war we had trouble with a bunch of nigger soldiers that were shipped into our training camps from the North and East. But they weren't our niggers. They hadn't been raised up right.

It is a fact, however, that we have no such race riots in the South as have been staged lately in Washington, D.C., Boston, Chicago, Omaha, East St. Louis and Tulsa. Why? We started right. We gave the "cullud" element to understand a long time ago, what we expected out of them in the shape of good behavior. Now and then a "bad nigger" develops himself into our special notice. When he does, we take him out and kill him. That's all. And that's the last of it.

Well-meaning folks in the northern states honestly feel that we people of the South are unjust and cruel in dealing with the Negro. They think it a shame that we don't have some nigger policemen patrolling the streets and telling the white men where to spit; they think it awful that a "cullud" lecturer on race-equality from Chicago can't come to Dallas and demand service in our hotels and restaurants, or sit by the side of our daughters in the theaters. Our friends of the North can go ahead and think whatever they please. We've got a plan that works! Our plan doesn't call for a race war every time we find it necessary to settle with one bad nigger.

To my mind, the aspiration of the Negro to sit by the side of the white man, in the councils of the white man's civilization is the very acme of impudence. In the world's six thousand years of history the Negro remained a beast in the woods and didn't even learn to cook his meat. He worshipped fire, thinking it was a god that feasted on dry sticks. The Negro produced no historian, even of his own long savagery. And in that night of savagery there gleams no star. The Negro, through sixty centuries, never wrote a book, never composed an opera, never painted a picture, never carved a statue, never sang a song that would grace music's kingly realm. White adventurers trapped him in his native jungles only a few years ago; shipped him in chains to serve the white man in other lands; a stroke of political fortune makes him "equal" to the white man in our country, and he has the consummate gall and impudence to want—a place at the council board of the white man's civilization.

It will never happen in Texas, gentlemen!

### APPENDIX E

Editorial comment in the Chicago *Defender*, September 6, 1919, entitled "Mr. Hoyne's Mistaken View."

State's Attorney Hoyne it seems is of the impression that black gamblers started the race riots in Chicago. Mr. Hoyne is mistaken. He fails absolutely to grasp the underlying causes in this community. When he charges our people with having brought on the disgraceful happenings centering about the first week of August, he flies in the face of the real facts.

Mr. Hoyne seems to have lost sight of a number of very disagreeable instances immediately preceeding [sic] the actual outbreak of hostilities between whites and blacks. He has forgotten evidently the repeated bombing of the houses of our citizens, resulting in the destruction of much valuable property. Likewise he overlooks the wanton and inexcuseable [sic] beatings of our people in Washington Park about the middle of June. His memory also proves false when he fails to call to mind that a black man was killed at 54th and Union Avenue, another at 51st and Wentworth Avenue, and still another at 57th and Lafayette Avenue. All of these things happened prior to the outbreaks of the latter part of July and the first of August.

Has our State's Attorney forgotten that not a single miscreant responsible for these murders has been apprehended? Is it to be wondered at that in the face of such laxity on the part of those charged with law enforcement that black citizens, in their alarm, should have sought and applied drastic measures for their own protection? While it is true that the hoodlum element may have been guilty of many overt acts, it is also true that the respectable element [sic] among our citizens were impelled to go outside of the law to protect themselves and their property when they could see no help from constituted authority.

We can easily understand the indictment of so many of our group. The conduct of the police force, in many instances, lends strong color to the suspicion that they were more or less in sympathy with the white rioters. It is only fair to deduce this from the fact that so many of our people were arrested in striking contrast to the arrest of the few white persons participating in the rioting. Even the grand jury, composed of some of Chicago's leaders in business and society, were forced to take note of this one-sided phase of the situation.

Much of the trouble can be laid at the door of the so-called athletic clubs west of Wentworth Avenue, from which, it appears, raiding parties were sent into the territory occupied by our people. Bands of these gangsters had swept through Washington Park and adjoining neighborhoods, attacking old and young alike. Several months ago we had occasion to call attention to these clubs as breeding spots for crime. And we believe we are safe in saying that much of the trouble leading up to the riots might have been avoided had these gang rendezvouses [sic] been closed. If our fighting State's Attorney would push his probe in the direction of these "clubs," he would go far toward striking at the real source of the race rioting in this community.

In this connection too much cannot be said in praise of the splendid body of men who made up the August grand jury. They were fearless in searching out and publishing the real truths. They were evidently imbued with a high sense of justice and determined to see fair play at all hazards. They were absolutely justified in their "strike," and an honest and fair investigation will reveal facts absolutely sustaining their position.

We are not condemning the State's Attorney for his attitude towards gambling houses and other disreputable resorts in the Second Ward. We believe as he does, that rotten political conditions are responsible for these evils. We know that for the last four or five years the Second Ward has been the dumping ground of much of Chicago's moral and social garbage, both white and black. And more power to his hand in any effort which he may make at cleaning it up. We must insist, however, that in his public statements of the cause of the riots he shows a woeful lack of information.

Editorial comment in the Chicago *Defender*, August 2, 1919, entitled "Reaping the Whirlwind."

The recent race riots at Washington resulting in the death of a number of white and black citizens, followed by similar occurrences in Chicago, are a disgrace to American civilization. One does not have to seek very far to find the underlying cause. It is not chargeable, as some writers think, to the general unrest now sweeping the world. Nor are we witnessing anything new in these disgraceful exhibitions of lawlessness. America is known the world over as the land of the lyncher and of the mobocrat. For years she has been sowing the wind and now she is reaping the whirlwind. The Black worm has turned. A Race that has furnished hundreds of thousands of the best soldiers that the world has ever seen is no longer content to turn the left cheek when smitten upon the right.

The younger generation of black men are not content to move along the line of least resistence [sic] as did their sires. For his awakening, however, the color madness of the American white man alone is responsible. Not content with inflicting upon him every form of humiliation that could be devised at home, he carried his infamous color propaganda to Europe. With the close of the war the returning soldiers brought back the most harrowing tales of abuses at the hands of the American military contingent. These stories have been carried broadcast over the land and have inflamed our people as few things could have done.

We have little sympathy with lawlessness, whether those guilty of it be black or white, but it cannot be denied that we have much in the way of justification for our changed attitude. Under the promise of a square deal our boys went cheerfully into the service of the country hoping that the aftermath of the struggle would find our people in an improved social and industrial condition. All of our speakers and writers held to this view and kept it consistently before our youth as an inducement to enlistment. Industrially our position has undoubtedly been benefited by the war. Socially it has grown decidedly worse. On all sides we have been made to feel the humiliating pressure of the white man's prejudice. In Washington it was a case of "teaching us our place." In Chicago it was a case of limiting our sphere to bounds that had neither the sanction of law nor sound common sense. In both cases we resented the assumption. Hence the race riots.

## MANUSCRIPTS

Davenport, Charles R. "The Knoxville Riot—August 30–31, 1919." Manuscript, University of Tennessee Archives, Knoxville, 1967.

## PUBLIC DOCUMENTS

National Commission on the Causes and Prevention of Violence June 1969. *Violence in America*. New York: The New American Library, 1969.

*The Supreme Court Reporter*. Vol. XLI. St. Paul: West Publishing Company, 1922.

Thompson, Frank M. *Reports of Cases Argued and Determined in the Supreme Court of Tennessee*. Vols. CXLIV and CXLV. Columbis, E. W. Stephens Publishing Company, 1921 and 1922.

U. S., *Congressional Record*. Vol. LVIII. (November 19, 1919).

## BOOKS

Alexander, Charles C. *The Ku Klux Klan in the Southwest*. Lexington: University of Kentucky Press, 1965.

Allen, Frederick L. *Only Yesterday*. New York: Harper and Brothers, 1931.

Cantril, Hadley. *The Psychology of Social Movements*. New York: John Wilen and Sons, 1941.

Carter, Paul A. *The Decline and Revival of the Social Gospel: Social and Political Liberalism in American*

*Protestant Churches, 1920–1940.* Ithaca: Cornell University Press, 1954.

Chalmers, David M. *Hooded Americanism: The History of the Ku Klux Klan.* Chicago: Quadrangle Books, 1968.

Chicago Commission on Race Relations. *The Negro in Chicago.* Chicago: University of Chicago Press, 1922.

Elliott, Mabel A., and Francis E. Merrill. *Social Disorganization.* New York: Harper and Brothers, 1961.

Ezell, John S. *The South Since 1865.* New York: The Macmillan Company, 1963.

Fishel, Leslie H., Jr., and Benjamin Quarles. *The Negro American: A Documentary History.* Glenview, Ill.: Scott, Foresman, 1967.

Gatewood, Williard B., Jr., *Controversy in the Twenties: Fundamentalism, Modernism, and Evolution.* Nashville: Vanderbilt University Press, 1969.

Jackson, Kenneth T. *The Ku Klux Klan in the City, 1915–1930.* New York: Oxford University Press, 1967.

Miller, Robert M. *American Protestantism and Social Issues, 1919–1939.* Chapel Hill: University of North Carolina Press, 1958.

Murray, Robert K. *Red Scare: A Study in National Hysteria, 1919–1920.* Minneapolis: University of Minnesota Press, 1953.

Myrdal, Gunnar. *An American Dilemma: The Negro Problem and Modern Democracy.* New York: Harper and Brothers, 1944.

Newby, I. A. *Jim Crow's Defense: Anti-Negro Thought in America, 1900–30.* Baton Rouge: Louisiana State University Press, 1967.

Simpson, George E., and J. Milton Yinger. *Racial and Cultural Minorities.* New York: Harper and Brothers, 1958.

Slosson, Preston W. *The Great Crusade and After, 1914–28*. New York: The Macmillan Company, 1930.

Spear, Allan H. *Black Chicago: The Making of a Negro Ghetto, 1890–1920*. Chicago: University of Chicago Press, 1967.

Sullivan, Mark. *Our Times: The United States, 1900–1925*. Vol. VI. New York: Charles Scribner's Sons, 1935.

Thompson, Edgar T., and Everett C. Hughes, eds. *Race: Individual and Collective Behavior*. Glencoe, Ill.: The Free Press, 1958.

van den Berghe, Pierre L. *Race and Racism: A Comparative Perspective*. New York: John Wiley and Sons, 1967.

Waskow, Arthur I. *From Race Riot to Sit-in: 1919 and the 1960's*. New York: Doubleday, 1966.

White, Walter F. *How Far the Promised Land?* New York: The Viking Press, 1956.

Woodward, C. Vann. *The Strange Career of Jim Crow*. New York: Oxford University Press, 1957.

### NEWSPAPERS

Chicago *Defender*, April 26, August 2, 9, September 6, December 27, 1919; January 1, February 28, 1920; July 30, August 20, 1921.

Knoxville *Journal and Tribune*, August 26, 31, September 1, 2, 1919.

Memphis *Commercial Appeal*, August 31, September 29, October 2, 3, 4, 1919; January 10, 1920; June 3, 1921.

*Nashville Banner*, August 31, 1919.

*New York Times*, September 1, 1919; June 2, 1921.

*New York World*, November 19, 1919.

*Johnson City* (Tennessee) *Staff*, May 14, 1919.

ARTICLES

"Blood and Oil," *Survey*, XLVI (June 11, 1921), 369–70.

Bullock, M. W. "What Does the Negro Want?" *Outlook*, CXXIII (September 17, 1919), 110.

Butts, J. W., and Dorothy James, "The Underlying Causes of the Elaine Riot of 1919," *Arkansas Historical Quarterly*, XX (1961), 95–104.

Comstock, Amy. " 'Over There', Another View of the Tulsa Riots," *Survey*, XLVI (July 2, 1919), 460.

Cox, Oliver C. "Lynching and the Status Quo," *Journal of Negro Education*, XIV (1945), 576–588.

"Darkest Cloud," *Survey*, XLII (August 2, 1919), 675–76.

Grimshaw, Allen D. "Lawlessness and Violence in America and Their Special Manifestations in Changing Negro-White Relationships," *Journal of Negro History*, XLIV (1959), 52–72.

Harmon, J. H., Jr. "The Negro as a Local Business Man," *Journal of Negro History*, XIV (1929), 116–55.

Haynes, George E. "Race Riots in Relation to Democracy," *Survey*, XLII (August 9, 1919), 697–99.

Holman, Charles W. "Race Riots in Chicago," *Outlook*, CXXII (August 13, 1919), 566–67.

Lasch, Christopher. "The Anti-Imperialists, The Philippines and the Inequality of Man," *Journal of Southern History*, XXIV (1958), 319–31.

"Law-And-Order Anarchy," *Nation*, CXIII (August 13, 1921), 113.

Lieberson, Stanley, and Arnold R. Silverman. "The Precipitants and Underlying Conditions of Race Riots," *American Sociological Review*, XXX (1965), 887–98.

Miller, E. E. "The War and Race Feeling," *Outlook*, CXXIII (September 10, 1919), 52 and 56.

Miller, Robert M. "The Protestant Churches and Lynching, 1919–1939," *Journal of Negro History*, XLII (1957), 118–31.

"Mob-Rule as a National Menace," *Literary Digest*, LXIII (October 18, 1919), 9–11.

"Moving Toward Race War," *New Republic*, XXVII (June 22, 1921), 96–97.

Mowry, George E., "The Twenties: The Limits of Freedom," in Richard W. Leopold, Arthur S. Link, and Stanley Coben (eds.). *Problems in American History*. Vol. II. Englewood Cliffs: Prentice-Hall, 1966.

"On the Firing-Line During the Chicago Race Riots," *Literary Digest*, LXII (August 23, 1919), 44–46.

"Race Riots in Washington and Chicago," *Current History*, X (September, 1919), 453–54.

"Racial Tension and Race Riots," *Outlook*, CXXII (August 6, 1919), 532–34.

Rogers, Ben R. "William E. B. DuBois, Marcus Garvey and Pan-Africa," *Journal of Negro History*, XL (1955), 154–65.

Rogers, O. A., Jr. "The Elaine Race Riots of 1919," *Arkansas Historical Quarterly*, XIX (1960).

Scarborough, W. S. "Race Riots and Their Remedy," *Independent and Weekly Review*, XCIX (August 16, 1919), 223.

Seligmann, Herbert J. "Protecting Southern Womanhood," *Nation*, CVIII (June 14, 1919), 938–39.

———. "Race War in Washington," *New Republic*, XX (August 13, 1919), 48–50.

———. "The Menace of Race Hatred," *Harper's Monthly Magazine*, CXL–CXLI (1920), 537–43.

———. "What is Behind the Negro Uprisings?" *Current Opinion*, LXVII (September, 1919), 154–55.

Taylor, Graham, "Chicago in the Nation's Race Strife," *Survey*, XLII (August 9, 1919), 695–97.

"The Lesson of Tulsa," *Outlook*, CXXVIII (June 15, 1921), 380–81.

"The Tulsa Race Riots," *Independent and Weekly Review*, CV (June 18, 1921), 646–47.

"Tulsa," *Nation*, CXII (June 15, 1921), 839.

Tuttle, William B., Jr. "Views of a Negro During the Red Summer of 1919—A Document," *Journal of Negro History*, LI (1966), 209–18.

"What the South Thinks of Northern Race-Riots," *Literary Digest*, LXII (August 16, 1919), 17–18.

White, Walter F. "Chicago and Its Eight Reasons," *Crisis*, (1919), 293–94.

———. "The Race Conflict in Arkansas," *Survey*, XLIII (December 13, 1919), 233–34.

———. "The Eruption of Tulsa," *Nation*, CXII (June 29, 1921), 909, 910.

"Why the Negro Appeals to Violence," *Literary Digest*, LXII (August 9, 1919), 11.

Lambert, Gerard B., Co., 39
Lee County, Arkansas, 38
Lee, Acting Police Captain
I. S., 77
Lieberson, Stanley, 18
Lilly, Orley R., 50
Lindsey, Mrs. Bertie, 22–23,
27
*Literary Digest*, 88
Lithuanians, 86
"Little Africa", 58, 59
Lovings, Joseph, 83
Lowden, Governor Frank,
82, 85
Lowe-Horde Hardware
Company, 31
Luttrell, S. B., and Company,
30
Lynching, 3, 6, 9–12

Market Harness and Hard-
ware Co., 31
Market Street, 31
Martin, John, 55
Massengill, Jim, 25
Maxwell Furniture Company,
31
Mays, Maurice, 24–27, 36, 108
Mays, William, 25
Memphis *Commercial Ap-
peal*, 109
McClung, C. M., and Co., 29
McCullough, Sheriff, 57–58
McHale, Patrick, 77
McMillan, Mayor John E.,
28, 105
Mercy Hospital, 82
Middleton, Detective Ser-
geant, 79
Missouri Pacific Railroad, 48
Monroe County, Arkansas, 38

Moore, Frank, 55
Murphy, Colonel George W.,
54

NAACP, 67, 110
National Guardsmen, 28
Nelson, Judge A. R., 36
New York *Times*, 90
"Niggertown," 60–61, 69, 70
Ninth Ward, 27

O'Brien, Policeman John F.,
79
Organization of the Progressive Farmers' and House-
hold Union of America,
The, 40–44, 51
"Our Flag", 87

Page, Sarah, 57
Payne, Lieutenant James W.,
33, 35
Phillips County, Arkansas,
38–39, 110, 112
Porter, W. L., 107
Potter Furniture Company,
31
Powell, V. E., 40
Prairie Avenue, 79
Pratt, Sheriff's Deputy
Charles, 45
Provident Hospital, 77

Racism, 3
Ragan, Frank, 77
"Ragan's Colts", 87
Rape, 10, 12, 18
Reconstruction, 6
Red Cross, 63, 86
Ridley, Saleb A., 71–72